The Leaders You Need

The Leaders You Need

How to Create Diverse Leadership Teams for a More Dynamic, Resilient Future

Karen Brown

The MIT Press
Cambridge, Massachusetts
London, England

The MIT Press would like 'to thank the anonymous peer reviewers who provided comments on drafts of this book. The generous work of academic experts is essential for establishing the authority and quality of our publications. We acknowledge with gratitude the contributions of these otherwise uncredited readers.

This book was set in ITC Stone Serif Std and ITC Stone Sans Std by New Best-set Typesetters Ltd. Printed and bound in the United States of America.

Library of Congress Cataloging-in-Publication Data

Names: Brown, Karen (DEI consultant), author.
Title: The leaders you need : how to create diverse leadership teams for a more
    dynamic, resilient future / Karen Brown.
Description: Cambridge, Massachusetts : The MIT Press, [2024] | Includes
    bibliographical references and index.
Identifiers: LCCN 2023057569 (print) | LCCN 2023057570 (ebook) |
    ISBN 9780262049085 (hardcover) | ISBN 9780262379519 (epub) |
    ISBN 9780262379502 (pdf)
Subjects: LCSH: Diversity in the workplace. | Leadership.
Classification: LCC HF5549.5.M5 B758 2024 (print) | LCC HF5549.5.M5 (ebook) |
    DDC 658.3008—dc23
LC record available at https://lccn.loc.gov/2023057569
LC ebook record available at https://lccn.loc.gov/2023057570

10 9 8 7 6 5 4 3 2 1

Leo Tolstoy wrote, "Nothing can make our life, or the lives of other people, more beautiful than perpetual kindness." This encapsulates the person to whom I dedicate this book: my father.

Though he only had a grade school education, he was highly principled, rich with wisdom, and adored by everyone who knew him. He practiced equity, equality, inclusion, and fairness every day, and I learned from him how to value the full range of humanity.

Contents

Introduction: A New Framework for Greater Diversity in Leadership

Talent is abundant. Opportunity is not.

I began writing this book in 2018, amid a global conversation about economic inequality and the recognition that society cannot prosper if it leaves people out. The world economy was stable. Yet, according to the United Nations, 70 percent of the world population lived in countries where wealth concentrated increasingly at the top. Women and ethnic minorities, no matter where they lived, were more likely to be poor than men in the majority.

You may ask what this has to do with a book about diversity in leadership. It's this: when decision-makers include individuals from varied economic backgrounds, generations, genders, races and ethnicities, sexual orientations, physical abilities, and religion, everyone is better off—employees, customers, suppliers, investors, and the people in the communities where businesses operate.

I have worked with global companies for over two decades to advance opportunities for people who are underrepresented in leadership. The diverse teams we built became stronger, more trusted, more resilient, and more innovative, and were therefore better prepared to create more value for their stakeholders. The argument that diversity, equity, and inclusion opponents often advance—that these efforts take opportunities away from better-qualified people in the majority group—have no basis in fact. Rather, by expanding the talent pool, you are likely to find equally or better-qualified people you have overlooked. According to one study by the London School of Economics, quotas to achieve gender parity (though a blunt instrument with mixed results) weed out unqualified men rather than promote unqualified women.[1] An effective approach to diversity is not a win-or-lose, zero-sum proposition.

We need strength from diversity more now than in our collective memory. Entire industries are struggling with increased economic uncertainty, culture wars, climate change, migration, and civil war. In the United States, horror over police brutality, revelations about sexual harassment, attacks on religious minorities, and rights-limiting legal rulings have renewed demands for gender, racial, religious, and LGBTQ+ equality.

Consumers are responding with their wallets, and employees with their energy. The Edelman Trust Barometer, a global study of consumer sentiment, finds that consumers prefer to work for, invest in, and do business with brands that reflect their values and beliefs. They also want companies to do more to solve societal problems including climate change, economic inequality, and systemic injustice.[2]

Potential Leaders Are Left Out

Organizations without leaders who represent the full range of humanity will find it hard to confront these demands or thrive in the long run. Anyone who manages people, whether directly or indirectly, has a role in creating a workplace where every employee has what they need to do their work and to excel.

Yet in the United States, the ranks of top leaders remain mostly male and White. Among CEOs, fewer than one-third are women, while fewer than 15 percent identify as Black, Hispanic, or Asian.[3] These groups are underrepresented in the role compared to their share of the total population. At the most elite level, the gap is starker. Only six CEOs in the 2022 Fortune 500 were Black; seventy-four were women. These were record highs.[4]

The homogeneity of business leadership does not occur because individuals representing a cross section of people lack potential. Rather, the way organizations develop and select managers and leaders—how they identify people with potential, give them opportunities to gain experience and build networks, and choose them for management roles—leaves people out. Since the dawn of capitalism, the world, including businesses, has been shaped primarily by and for White men. They have become the default for just about everything, from determining medication doses to what leaders should look and act like. Everyone else has been largely absent from decision-making roles where they could help to shape government policies, legal and economic systems, workplace rules, and our daily lives.

This book is not, however, about what is wrong with organizations; there are plenty of books on that subject. Nor is it about what is wrong with men, White people, straight people, or people with any characteristic that puts them in the majority. I am not here to lecture, blame, or shame anyone into action. I am a problem solver. I want to help organizations—whether large or small, for-profit or nonprofit—get the leaders they need by building stronger, smarter teams.

An Approach That Works

Many organizations treat diversity, equity, and inclusion as a numbers exercise. Leaders have good intentions, set diversity goals, and track progress toward them—then become frustrated when they do not achieve them. We need to set goals to know what we are accomplishing. But I have learned that the best way to close the gap between an organization's ambitions and its results is to focus less on counting heads and more on making heads count. The ABCD framework that I developed and use with my clients will help you discover who is missing in your management and leadership ranks, and what to do about it.

The framework comprises four pillars, each of which has its own chapter:

A—Align diversity, equity, and inclusion with business priorities
B—Build strong partnerships with stakeholders
C—Cultivate a culture of role models
D—Define objectives and outcomes with data

Additional chapters advise how to dismantle the barriers to implementing the framework and become a more inclusive people leader. Each chapter includes questions to guide your journey.

I will not prescribe programs or policies. Instead, I will give you a foundation to create a culture in your team, your department, your division, or your organization that welcomes the full range of humanity. This book plants the seeds for understanding what you need to do to embed diversity, equity, and inclusion in how you identify, develop, and select the people who will become managers and leaders.

Asking questions is fundamental to solving any challenge—a lesson I have learned from a life of travel. In every new place, I build relationships and settle into a new environment by being curious and learning as much as I can about the people around me. My curiosity about humanity has led me to almost eighty countries on six continents, including many places where I didn't speak the local language. I lean into other skills—listening and patience—to help me connect and communicate. I have learned to be less judgmental, to see what is unfamiliar to me not as right or wrong, but different.

As you might guess, I have amassed a network of friends and colleagues around the world. That's not why I share this story. I share it because through these experiences, putting people first has become second nature. Understanding who they are, what they care about, and what they need so they can give me what I need is my default as a human being and the basis for my work. You don't have to travel the world to gain these skills and absorb them into your psyche. All it takes to start is curiosity about the people on your team and a commitment to acting on what you learn.

Unprecedented Opportunity

We cannot wait any longer to elevate a more diverse set of leaders. Multiple crises this decade have highlighted many ways that our public institutions and businesses poorly serve women, racial and ethnic minorities, LGBTQ+ people, people with disabilities, and those with neurological differences. There are myriad reasons we are in this situation—and myriad remedies for it—that are beyond this book. But every organization, whether it exists to make money or serve a mission, is designed to harness talent to solve problems. By doing so, it fills society's unmet needs. Therefore, leaders and managers have unprecedented opportunities to chart their organization's future.

Intrinsic aspects of our identities determine how we experience the world and have a powerful influence on what we expect, how we think, and what we want. A more diverse set of leaders and managers will have a more comprehensive vision for how to meet customers' needs. The diversity of thought and experiences that we say we value and need is inseparable from the varied traits that make us who we are. We won't get the full range of perspectives and ideas from our teammates unless we include every dimension of their human diversity. Anyone who does, wins.

However, talented people continue to be overlooked for leadership and management roles because their organizations do not account for the influence that people leaders have on who rises through management. Landing a leadership position is neither guaranteed nor accidental. People advance because someone higher ranking is aware of their talent and career goals and gives them the green light—for example, including them in groups where they can get to know other decision-makers; placing them in roles where they can develop; and recommending, considering, and appointing them to more senior positions.

And yet, because of lingering stereotypes, ingrained social behavior, uncertainty about how to address race and gender without creating discord, or simple inertia, the people whose careers superiors nurture continue to be predominantly men, and, in Western companies, they are White. These embedded patterns can change. Many leaders and managers want to change them. However, they need to be convinced they can succeed at what they may fear will be uncomfortable work.

With positive and pragmatic steps such as those I offer in this book, you can act decisively to build more diverse, inclusive leadership teams. My approach will help you appoint leaders and managers who represent the abundance of backgrounds, experiences, and characteristics of your workforce, customers, and community of stakeholders. And they will contribute their talents to ensuring your business can compete and flourish in new ways.

1 Why Diversity Programs Don't Work—and What Does

The proliferation of books and articles about diversity in business makes a powerful case that organizations with diverse leadership and management teams perform better. And yet, many diversity initiatives continue to be driven by the same three factors: compliance with legal mandates; a sense of social justice; and the need to appease customers, business partners, employees, and other stakeholders with numbers. Although these are critical and necessary motivators, they are not enough. If they were, we would have a more diverse set of executives and managers on every board and management team. Meanwhile, without leaders and managers who represent the full range of humanity, organizations are leaving on the table ideas, knowledge, and expertise that would strengthen them and make them more successful.

Consider, for example, that women control or influence how to invest around one-third of global wealth—an estimated $81 trillion or more in 2023—as well as the vast majority of consumer purchasing decisions.[1] Yet women tell researchers the marketplace does not serve them well. A decade ago, a six-nation study of investors by the Center for Talent Innovation found that 53 percent of women did not have financial advisors. Among those that did, two-thirds reported their advisors didn't understand them. Women were most satisfied with advisors who had "gender smarts"—who understood women's time constraints, investment goals, and other needs that differed from those of men. The researchers concluded financial services firms could only deliver what female investors want by providing leadership that "embodies and embraces diversity in order to foment an inclusive culture where women contribute their ideas and socialize their gender smarts. Inclusive cultures drive bottom-line growth on two fronts: female employees innovate a business model that connects the firm to female investors, and female investors are more inclined to invest in firms with diversity in senior leadership."[2]

Top executives usually can't make this case, however, because they approach diversity, equity, and inclusion as a set of programs designed to target a specific population (e.g., women, racial and ethnic minorities) rather than as a method for discovering and capitalizing on the talent that they need to achieve business outcomes. They count people and check boxes to keep lawyers and activists at bay. They aren't looking for ways to ensure that every employee can excel—even though developing the most talented employees is critical to filling the pipeline of future managers and leaders.

HR professionals may promote the idea that diversity, equity, and inclusion help with corporate reputation or recruitment, but even then, they don't tie them to any specific business purpose, and most employees don't make the connection, either. According to one global study of companies by the consultancy PwC, 80 percent of respondents reported the primary goal for these initiatives was something other than achieving business results.[3]

The twin underpinnings of corporate diversity, equity, and inclusion efforts—legal compliance and moral duty—practically guarantee that they won't get the attention they're due. Positioning talent development as an obligation may be the surest way to accord it the minimum resources and attention.

Meanwhile, although many leaders and managers believe in equality, they do not always know how to connect it with making money or fostering an engaged workforce. They may not be aware of the link between social justice and business success. Or they may be averse to associating them because they think it unseemly to make moral or ethical decisions on the basis of profitability. But there is no way around the fact that people make the customer experience sweet or sour, people do the work, people achieve results, and leaders and managers decide who those people are. I have never met an executive or manager who does not want to assemble the best possible team. They will get it if they approach their strategy and objectives through the lens of diversity, equity, and inclusion and put people—all people—at the heart of everything they do.

A top leadership team that represents the full range of humanity sends a powerful signal that the organization welcomes and values all people as employees, customers, and community members. This is important inside an organization to show employees that they each can exercise their talents and pursue their ambitions.

Increasingly, leaders also view their efforts to advance diversity, equity, and inclusion in management as essential to attracting new hires, gaining customers, and maintaining the organization's license to operate. We can see this at work in organizations' efforts to include people from a more diverse range of demographic characteristics and backgrounds on their boards of directors, as well as in advertising that includes more Black and brown faces. In the United States, where I am writing, we may also see it in public statements from high-profile CEOs who support voting rights and racial justice.

And while it may be tempting to be cynical about the commitment behind such steps, I see momentum. Forward-looking leaders see our interconnected, multiethnic, multicultural, multigenerational future and know they will not be as successful in the long run if they do not embrace it and stand up for it. By appointing leaders and managers who embody this future, they make their organizations ready to meet it.

Defining Diversity, Equity, and Inclusion

Before we continue, let's define *diversity*, *equity*, and *inclusion*. Everyone may not understand these terms in the same way as they relate to the workplace and employment.

Diversity is everyone's inherent and acquired traits. People are born with and acquire a variety of characteristics during their lives. These include physical abilities (such as sight, hearing, and mobility), social identities (such as gender, race, ethnicity, age, class, and sexual orientation), and personal attributes (such as expertise, values, religion, ethnicity, and education). Notice that this definition describes the world. It is more expansive than we often assume in American popular discourse—as shorthand for people who are not White or male. It encompasses the full range of distinctions and differences among people.

Equity is meeting the needs of everyone. Those inherent and acquired characteristics lead to different needs for individuals and groups who share them. Therefore, equity requires we distribute resources and benefits based on what people need. It also demands our practices and policies be just, transparent, and consistent. Equity differs from *equality*, which refers to individuals or groups having the same rights, status, and opportunities to be treated the same, or to be judged according to the same standards. When we focus on equity, we pay attention to whether all people and groups have access to the resources or accommodations they need to participate in the workplace as equals, and we design solutions to ensure they do.

Inclusion is maximizing all human traits. In the workplace, people's differences are an advantage when they help their colleagues achieve their goals. Some people may also need accommodations to best utilize their talents. When managers are inclusive, they think about the traits of all the people on their teams and how to create an atmosphere where everyone can participate without feeling inhibited by their differences. No one is ostracized or punished because they differ from the group that constitutes the majority.

Because these three words—*diversity*, *equity*, and *inclusion*—are often used together, people may think of them as encompassing a single activity. But as you can see, they refer to distinct goals. I want you to keep this in mind as you read. The only exception is when I talk about diversity, equity, and inclusion as a business function because there is only one of those in an organization.

What's Wrong with Compliance

Though we have been working on diversity, equity, and inclusion for over sixty years, we haven't come far from where we started. The impetus for modern efforts—the civil rights legislation of the mid-1960s—largely explains why. I won't take you through the entire history. Know this: whether executives at the time felt a moral obligation to foster equality (and certainly some did), they took steps to comply with the law. When companies were sued for discrimination, they could often avoid multimillion dollar penalties and court-directed remedies to their employment and management practices if they were attempting to do better. This has passed for decades as a business rationale for investing in such programs as equal-opportunity hiring, leadership development programs for women and racial and ethnic minorities, and antibias and sexual harassment training. But it's hardly an inspiring one, as research shows.

Sociologists Frank Dobbin and Alexandra Kalev have documented the many ways that corporate diversity and antidiscrimination programs have fallen short, and even undermined companies' commitments to diversity, equity, and inclusion. "Companies have been trying to fix inequality at work by finding bias in the hearts, and actions, of individual managers," they write. "That has been a spectacular failure. It turns out to be more effective to focus on bias and discrimination in systems than in people. What we need to do is to democratize corporate career systems—to open them up to groups that have been excluded."[4]

I couldn't agree more. We are unlikely to eradicate exploitation, mistreatment, or bias from the human condition. We will always need to encourage and enforce acceptable behavior and address violations. But programs that are focused on keeping companies out of court don't ask managers to rethink how they hire, develop, and promote people absent evidence they have acted improperly. Nor do they contribute to establishing a culture that respects all employees and values everyone's contribution. Instead, they treat managers, especially the (mostly White) men who make most personnel decisions in US companies, as if they are the problem and consider fixing them to be the solution. Year upon year, managers attend mandatory diversity training where they are told to change their behavior rather than to scrutinize the systems and incentives—or the lack of them—that perpetuate the status quo.

Meanwhile, what most managers and employees know about diversity, equity, and inclusion is limited to numbers: the percentage of women or racial and ethnic minorities in staff and management roles. A focus on numbers contributes to the belief that people from underrepresented groups are appointed to fill quotas (whether or not this is actually true) rather than because they are the most-qualified people for their roles. And so, the programs foment resentment. As reported by CNBC, a 2017 survey by consultancy EY found that about a third of men believed their workplaces excluded them and blamed corporate programs to increase diversity as one factor.[5]

Even people who believe in equality in the abstract may think they are being blamed or excluded by diversity programs. In a hiring simulation, psychologists Tessa Dover, Brenda Major, and Cheryl Kaiser found White male recruits who were told about a fictional company's pro-diversity policies were more likely to believe the firm would discriminate against Whites, compared to White males who didn't get pro-diversity messages in their recruiting materials. These beliefs affected how the men performed in interviews. They behaved as if threatened. "Importantly, diversity messages led to these effects regardless of these men's political ideology, attitudes toward minority groups, beliefs about the prevalence of discrimination against Whites, or beliefs about the fairness of the world," the authors explain in a *Harvard Business Review* article about the study. "This suggests just how widespread negative responses to diversity may be among White men: the responses exist even among those who endorse the tenets of diversity and inclusion."[6]

The Right Thing Isn't Enough

Executives may in fact believe that creating a diverse, equitable, and inclusive workforce is the right thing to do, but belief doesn't make quarterly earnings. Middle managers, who are executors of everything that comes from above, may have the same beliefs, but they don't always see how they connect with day-to-day reality. What does diversity have to do with the report due on Friday, the sales goals at the end of the month, or the person who didn't show up for their shift? How does anyone make their team more diverse when they are cutting costs and laying people off?

Research tells us that moral suasion isn't enough to sustain our attention. A series of experiments by economists Ernesto Dal Bó and Pedro Dal Bó found that giving people a moral rationale made them more likely to cooperate than if they were given no reason at all. But their level of cooperation—measured by how much money participants contributed to a joint "investment account" with a partner—declined over multiple rounds of the experiment. The study found greater, and more sustained, cooperation when participants were told they could be punished for not contributing the suggested amount, but even then, the contributions diminished in later rounds.

Interestingly, participants' expectations of each other played a significant role in their behavior. Those who had a moral rationale were more likely to cooperate when they thought others got the same message.[7] Other research on what motivates people to do the right thing similarly observes that as social beings, we tend to behave how others expect us to—that is, according to the norms in our environment.

This—our wish to do what others expect—is at the heart of what is missing from most corporate diversity, equity, and inclusion efforts. Whatever their good intentions, managers will manage according to what their organizations expect of them. And they know what they are expected to do by what they're held accountable for. Unless they can see that creating an inclusive work environment and developing diverse leadership talent will help them meet their objectives, most won't make it a priority.

Sallie Krawcheck is CEO of the investment firm Ellevest, which is focused on increasing women's wealth. Prior to launching Ellevest, she was a senior executive at the financial services firms Citi and Merrill Lynch. During a 2019 interview on *The Daily Show* with Trevor Noah, she observed, "I do think CEOs really believe in the power of diversity."[8] But the same leaders are reluctant to tell managers how to make personnel decisions that would lead to diverse leadership. "When it comes time to promote the next person," they might say, "'Well, I think I read some research one time about diversity drives better results, but that young man, who reminds me so darn much of myself when I was younger, I just feel like he is going to do a better job,'" she said. In other words, managers are told they need to hire, develop, and promote a diverse slate of people. And they may agree that it's the right thing to do. But rarely are they told how to do it or given the tools they need, and rarely is the case made for why it matters in connection to their day-to-day duties.

To get results, top leaders need to think about what will help each manager change how they lead their people, as did Anna Brown, the former chief inclusion and diversity officer at Baker McKenzie. She describes "looking at each of our offices in each of our regions and approaching them very much on a bespoke basis" to establish goals for developing a more diverse pool of leaders, define how managers would be measured, and determine the resources and tools they would need.[9]

Here is where the framework comes in. The four pillars of the framework provide an approach to embedding diversity, equity, and inclusion in the daily decisions that leaders and managers make.

A—Align diversity, equity, and inclusion with business priorities

B—Build strong partnerships with stakeholders

C—Cultivate a culture of role models

D—Define objectives and outcomes with data

Whether you are a factory supervisor or the CEO, this framework will give you the power to maximize the talent on your team and change your organization.

Although every team, function, and department should be engaged if diversity, equity, and inclusion are to flourish, there is no single path to

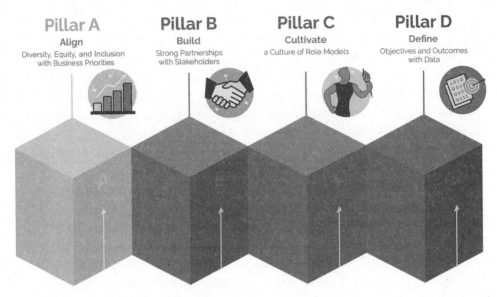

Figure 1.1
The four pillars of the ABCD framework provide an approach to embedding diversity, equity, and inclusion in the daily decisions that leaders and managers make.

success. Each business will, because of its industry, history, and culture, make its own way.

Some of my advice applies most directly to senior leaders. In such cases, others can learn what to expect from their top leadership team and what to ask for if they don't see it. It is already what we do to understand acceptable practices for ethics, safety, risk management, and financial audits.

Any leader or manager can be a diversity, equity, and inclusion champion, even when the organization as a whole has not embraced these efforts. You can use the framework to think through how and why diversity is important to the success of your team or unit. When you apply it to creating a welcoming and inclusive work environment and nurturing the abilities of everyone on your team, you will help your organization to achieve its business goals. And you can light the way forward for your colleagues.

Make Diversity, Equity, and Inclusion a Guiding Principle

What happens when you elevate diversity, equity, and inclusion from a compliance or moral exercise to a guiding principle for your organization?

We learned firsthand at Sodexo two decades ago when we were building what became a hugely successful and highly lauded diversity and inclusion program. In 2002 our then CEO, Michel Landel, decided the company should address the issues raised by a pending lawsuit that accused it of discriminating in promotion decisions. Landel believed that when every employee felt the company valued their contributions, they could be fully engaged in their work, and the company would be more successful. He wanted to do what was necessary to ensure that every employee could use all their talents and achieve their career goals.

Over time, Sodexo showed Landel was correct. In 2018 the company reported data from over fifty thousand managers worldwide, finding that business entities with "near equal" representation of women and men in leadership had higher operating margins and were more successful at retaining clients. When it surveyed employees two years later, 80 percent of respondents agreed that the company supported diversity in the workplace, and 69 percent agreed their managers enabled them "to thrive and be fulfilled at work."[10]

At the beginning, we made a mistake by tying part of managers' bonuses to achieving the diversity goals for their teams. Managers needed to be held accountable, but we hadn't built the support system they needed to learn how to identify, develop, and select women or racial and ethnic minorities— and, most importantly, why our business needed them to do so. We were still creating training and materials to help managers ask better (and unbiased) questions in interviews and conduct performance reviews that focused on employees' concrete accomplishments and goals instead of supervisors' opinions about employees' personalities. We had not explained how managers could see beyond their preconceived ideas about the qualities and experiences of promising leaders when they identified high-potential talent. And we could not yet describe in detail how diverse teams would help our business because we had not yet fully developed those arguments. Understandably, the managers and senior executives, who had up to 25 percent of their bonuses connected to their diversity targets, were displeased. They thought the process by which they were being evaluated was wrong, and they worried that the company was exposing itself to risks, such as lawsuits by managers who perceived that they were unfairly denied their bonuses.

We gained traction when we connected diversity and inclusion with the business goal of retaining our clients. Sodexo provides business services in a variety of industries, including food service, equipment maintenance, and housekeeping. We knew that when every employee felt they were treated justly, that managers valued their work, and that they could pursue a path to leadership if they had that goal, they would be motivated to do their best work for our clients.

Our program helped us to retain more clients—and gain new business—in an unexpected way as well. When we began, Sodexo was a pioneer in its approach to diversity and inclusion. Clients who faced their own struggles to create inclusive organizations turned to us for advice, which we gave freely. At one point, Sodexo provided pro bono consulting to clients who wanted to learn about our approach, and people flocked to sessions about our diversity and inclusion work at our annual client meetings. The company attributes about $1 billion in revenue to these efforts to help clients over time.[11]

Chapter 2 explores the first pillar of the framework. It shows you how to take the critical first step to creating more diverse leadership and management teams by connecting diversity, equity, and inclusion to why your organization exists and how you fulfill that purpose.

Chapter 3 covers the second pillar: building strong partnerships with stakeholders. It will help you identify the people whose influence and support you need, learn what it will take to influence them, and figure out what they need to support you.

We all need to feel our work means something to be engaged and do our best. One study found that when middle managers believe their work has a purpose and management has provided a clear vision and explicit expectations, firms perform better financially.[12] Employees who feel their employer shares their values are more likely to help their colleagues.[13] Furthermore, productivity can suffer when there is a mismatch between what leaders say they value and what they do.[14]

There is a debate about the purpose of a corporation in society: Should it focus on maximizing profits for shareholders or should it practice *stakeholder capitalism* and serve the interests of its customers, suppliers, employees, and local communities, too? In 2019 the Business Roundtable, a club of large-company CEOs, made headlines when 181 CEOs pledged support for the latter view.[15] Critics can question the sincerity of statements like these, absent evidence of specific actions or results. And it's true that CEOs are not starry-eyed idealists, progress does not happen overnight, and the pull of the status quo can be powerful. But the Business Roundtable members articulated a set of values that are both important to society and essential to their organizations' success in the long run. They appeared to put people—what they want, need, and contribute to every area where a company creates value—at the heart of profit making.[16] In doing so, they opened the door to making diversity, equity, and inclusion central tenets not only of how they manage talent but of how they do business.

Bruce Boyd, cofounder and principal of Arabella Advisors, describes how he views the connection: "We, in a very explicit way, hold everyone accountable to our values, and that's part of our periodic review: How are you performing against the firm's values?"[17] The company advises philanthropists on making grants and investments that support social and policy changes, such as closing the racial wealth gap, improving global health care, and addressing the effects of climate change. Boyd and his cofounder decided to invest in diversity, equity, and inclusion in part because "being advisors to philanthropists and helping them make a difference on issues they care about, which almost always directly affect Black and brown communities, while not having Black and brown voices at the table and partners in guiding that journey, seemed like a huge gap."

Arabella Advisors is a B corporation, which means social purpose is part of its charter. And yet, even though they made a professional commitment to creating a more equitable society, Boyd and his leadership team had to decide to connect this mission with how they managed their talent, operations, and processes. In this regard, the firm does not differ from any other business, and Boyd does not differ from any other senior executive who agrees, in principle, that diversity, equity, and inclusion are both morally right and drive better business decisions. Arabella Advisors' pursuit of equity extends to decisions such as which vendors supply food at company events, which bankers hold its earnings, who participates in their grant-making processes, and even whether to part ways with clients who don't share its vision. "We look for partners who bring the kind of commitment to their work that we bring to ours," Boyd says. "That has been an important shift, for sure."

A decade after making the commitment, "I wouldn't say we're 100 percent there; we will never be," he continues. "It's one thing to make a commitment to be a more diverse, inclusive, and equitable place. It's another to actually make it happen. And making it happen requires a sustained, serious commitment over a long period. Well, forever. And without that, it's really just window dressing."

Become a Role Model

As Boyd's comments suggest, aligning diversity, equity, and inclusion with the business's aims enables them to become ingrained in the culture. The example and efforts of managers, starting at the top, are critical to getting it to stick. CEOs and other top leaders are models for every behavior that managers are supposed to emulate. In diversity, equity, and inclusion, they have to set an example of how to lead a team inclusively, and they must establish the practices managers will follow for identifying and nurturing talent. Neither they nor middle and frontline managers can do this alone, however, and expect to sustain change. They need strong partnerships with business-savvy diversity, equity, and inclusion and HR leaders to guide them and the organization.

Only when leaders and managers walk the talk on diversity, equity, and inclusion, provide the tools for change, and use them will they be able to convince their colleagues and teammates they are sincere and should be followed. Chapter 4, which covers the third pillar of the framework, shows you how to cultivate a culture of role models. It explains what a welcoming and inclusive culture looks like, and how leaders can demonstrate behaviors that will transform the business culture. You'll find advice for breaking down the barriers that stand in the way of such a culture in chapter 6. Chapter 7 offers a guide for exploring how to engage with your team as an inclusive people leader.

Ask Who Is Missing

One practice is fundamental to every part of the framework, and that is learning how to look at your workforce, the leaders on your team, and (if you have a senior role) the leaders across the organization through the lens of diversity, equity, and inclusion. You cannot create leadership and management teams that are representative of your workforce, your customers, and your other stakeholders unless you ask, Who is missing? And why aren't more of them here? whenever you make decisions.

When you ask these questions, you are gaining insight into your blind spots. We all have them. Being aware of them is fundamental to seeing the possibilities for yourself, the people you manage, and your organization. Your workforce and business data can help you identify those blind spots and discover hidden opportunities for including more diverse leaders and managers. Chapter 5 focuses on this fourth element of the ABCD framework.

From Awareness to Action

Here are three examples from business and government that illustrate what leaders who commit to diversity, equity, and inclusion can do when they are aware of who is missing from their teams, know why they need a more diverse set of leaders and managers to achieve their goals, and have support from their stakeholders. The leaders in each case are CEOs, or the equivalent, with much power and influence. If you are not a senior leader, think of them as role models whose behavior you can adapt to your own scope of decision-making.

First, Procter & Gamble. When Robert McDonald became chairman and CEO of the consumer products manufacturer in 2009, he observed that women weren't well represented on the board of directors or in the company's management. Further, "whatever measure of diversity you want to choose, we were seeking equal representation of our customer base in our leadership. Because if you're trying to improve the lives of the people you're serving, you stand a better chance of doing that if you have employees who represent those people and *can* represent those people."[18] Rising through the ranks at P&G, McDonald had long embraced these values. And he acted on them. "It just wasn't a matter of changing anybody's mind or changing philosophy," because diversity was fundamental to the company and ingrained in its business practices. "I just said, 'Well, let's do it.'" Within a few years, the P&G board was about equally represented by women and men.

Two widely publicized examples from government illustrate some additional ways to think about the issue. Whatever your political party affiliation

> You cannot create leadership and management teams that are representative of your workforce, your customers, and your other stakeholders unless you ask, Who is missing? And why aren't more of them here? whenever you make decisions.

might be, I invite you to put it aside for a moment to consider, first, the approach that President Joe Biden took to appointing his leadership team, and next, the steps taken by Utah senator Mitt Romney, the former presidential candidate, to include women when he was governor of Massachusetts.

Biden chose a female vice president, Kamala Harris, and in 2021 appointed a racially and ethnically diverse cabinet that was 45 percent female—eleven women out of twenty-four cabinet secretaries. No previous president had appointed a cabinet this inclusive, regardless of party. As an NPR story noted, Biden found qualified female and non-White candidates for these roles: 95 percent of his appointees had prior government experience.[19] Had he wanted to emphasize corporate experience, he would have been able to find women and non-White leaders with that as well. Biden focused on assembling a group of leaders with as broad an array of experiences as possible to help him run the country, which is more gender and racially diverse than ever before. His actions made clear he was aware of this, that he accepted and acknowledged it as fact, and he took action to appoint a team that reflects the entire country that he leads.

He also directed his team to fill senior roles in federal agencies with candidates from historically underrepresented communities. Among 1,500 political appointees—roles that are roughly analogous to functional and line-of-business leaders in the private sector—58 percent were women. An executive order issued in June 2021 further instructed all agencies to review whether people from underrepresented communities who work for the federal government "face barriers to employment, promotion or professional development."[20]

Again, put aside your political lens and contemplate that this approach to leadership and talent development is similar to what many organizations do, and that CEOs take these steps for the same reasons as the president. Whether you are serving constituents in a diverse nation or a diverse set of business customers, having greater diversity among people in leadership will help you to achieve your goals. But you will not find them if you go about looking for leaders the same way and in the same places you always have. The fact is that geniuses come in all forms and live globally, in every city and postal code.

Now let's look at Romney, who was the Republican nominee for president in 2012. He was mocked for saying he had "binders full of women" when he was hiring for his cabinet as governor of Massachusetts. According to the

Boston Globe, Romney wanted to consider women, and his transition team in 2002 received two hundred résumés collected by a coalition of women's groups.[21] (There is some dispute about whether they asked for them or received them unsolicited but, regardless, Romney's interest in appointing women was known.) During the 2012 campaign, late-night comedians and meme creators thought Romney's remark belittling, and they criticized him for the apparent absence of women in his network. However, he was ultimately praised for the number of women he appointed to his cabinet as governor. As awkward as the effort and his description of it might seem, Romney got results because he drew from an expanded pool of talent.

Within an organization, what executives and managers do to advance diversity, equity, and inclusion helps to determine the pool of talent they have to draw from in their own organizations. Who you hire, develop, and recommend for promotion determines the composition of leaders at the level where you have influence. It doesn't matter how many diversity programs and inclusion initiatives you have: without making yourself aware of your blind spots and committing to bringing out the best from all your talent, a more diverse, inclusive leadership team and pipeline will be next to impossible to achieve or sustain.

Start by focusing on what you and your team are trying to achieve.

The ABCD Framework

2 Pillar A: How to Align Diversity, Equity, and Inclusion with Business Priorities

In 2020, the bank Citi calculated that the US economy had missed out on $16 trillion in GDP over the previous two decades because of discrimination against Blacks in wages, mortgages, education, and business lending. It estimated that closing these gaps would contribute an additional $4.8 trillion within five years.[1]

The big numbers are the sum of gains by millions of individual businesses that produce goods and services. As with many similar reports and academic studies before and since, researchers connected better financial performance with having a diverse workforce and leadership. Companies could help close the gaps, the report concluded, if their leaders backed diversity, equity, and inclusion initiatives, appointed more Black board members, and otherwise addressed racial imbalances. And, the research implied, companies would improve their performance.

Whether the goal is to increase profits, serve more people, or improve society, the correlation between having diverse leaders and achieving better performance can motivate many business leaders by connecting diversity, equity, and inclusion with their fiduciary responsibility. In addition, employees find their work more meaningful when the organization aspires to goals beyond merely making money. They are more likely to trust leaders who inspire them to a morally elevating purpose, such as delivering value to customers or serving the needs of all stakeholders.[2]

If leaders believe in the moral case for diversity, equity, and inclusion, connecting it with their business plan can make them more confident that they can pursue it in a way that motivates their workforce and improves the organization. If they have been closed-minded or indifferent, the opportunity to align diversity, equity, and inclusion with a business objective may get their attention.

However, understanding that greater diversity in leadership and management can lead to higher performance differs from knowing why and how it matters to your organization specifically. Even companies in the same industry may face distinct challenges in advancing underrepresented talent into leadership, and they will pursue this goal in different ways. Therefore, the first step in any effort to diversify demographic representation in leadership is to understand how the composition of your teams affects the ability of your organization to achieve its objectives.

"I started with the end in mind. What's the objective of the organization?" says Tracey Gray-Walker, CEO of AVMA Trust, which provides access to insurance coverage for veterinarians. Earlier in her career, Gray-Walker served as an operations executive and then as chief diversity officer for AXA in North America, followed by a commercial leadership role. She would say, "Let's look at all of those components that are going to help you with reaching your strategic objectives or goals . . . and let's show you how you can do this through an inclusive lens."[3]

The talent strategy for your organization should include a set of skills, competencies, and experiences that it will need in the future. If you are struggling to identify employees with the potential to develop these skills, and the people who get opportunities for leadership development primarily have the same demographic characteristics, there is a case for (1) identifying the open leadership and management positions in the organization and considering talented people from groups who are not currently well represented in these roles when filling them, and (2) examining whether the way you evaluate your direct reports causes you to overlook people who show promise as future leaders. We'll talk more about these steps later, but I would like you to keep them in mind as we delve into the connection between greater leadership diversity and business priorities.

We must wake up and see the full range of humanity walking among us. We must see the market and mission-fulfillment possibilities for what they are and not what they used to be. And we must see these as economic opportunities.

Know How Diversity Drives Your Business

Each time I start with an organization, my first step is to learn what drives it. Then I work with leaders to first look deeply and critically at their business

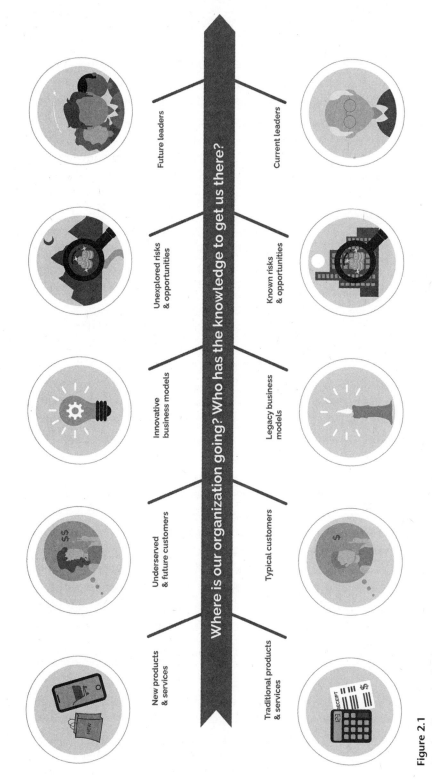

Figure 2.1

A more diverse leadership and management team positions an organization to recognize new opportunities, respond to developing customer needs, and understand risks.

goals or mission, the people they serve, and the values they and the organization espouse, and then to notice where representation is lacking.

This may be a new way of thinking. Most leaders and managers do not routinely consider whose perspective and experience is missing from their decisions. When they are filling a role, they might consider candidates with a variety of skills and work experience. But they don't regularly investigate whose perspective they need to include on their team, or why. They are frequently surprised to learn about their blind spots. However, you are simply adding another dimension to your decisions about the skills and abilities you need in your workforce and leading your teams. You are ensuring that the people you hire or develop internally for leadership and management roles are not only the best people you can find, with the skills and abilities you need, but also representative of your workforce, your customers, and the markets where you operate.

Some business priorities may not, at first glance, appear to require more diverse leadership, so be prepared to dig—and even question your own assumptions about them. For example, an early insight I had about Monsanto came from a conversation with Michael Frank, the executive in charge of international operations. As a senior leader, he was responsible for corporate diversity and inclusion mandates, and he asked me for help with appointing more women to his leadership team. Knowing that his customers were almost exclusively male, I told him I didn't immediately see a business problem that necessitated more women. Then he offered that many of his customers preferred doing business with women because they found them to be more empathetic and better listeners. He also shared that the influencers behind the decisions of many of his male customers were women.

Having scratched only a little below the surface, I could see he had a case. Frank had observed the connection between his business priorities— creating a better experience for customers and stronger relationships with them—and the need for women leaders. I helped him articulate that need in clear business terms to prove to himself that the goal was valid and to convince the rest of his team that it was worth the work required to achieve it.

Every organization needs this level of thinking from its leaders and managers. You can do it no matter how big your team is or how broad or narrow your scope of responsibility. You will know which priorities to focus on by inspecting the goals that your organization has defined as strategic and identifying which of them you are accountable for. Most leaders and managers have a role in achieving at least one of the following five priorities that serve top-line or bottom-line growth, or contribute to the mission, and that are common to most organizations today. These are:

- creating better customer experiences
- igniting innovation
- responding to business change
- building and maintaining a good corporate reputation
- managing risk and making smarter bets

You can pursue greater diversity in leadership based on any or all of these, depending, again, on your specific objectives and responsibilities.

The rest of this chapter explains how each of the five priorities connects with diversity, equity, and inclusion.

Creating Better Customer Experiences

What if the people who green-lighted films made more movies that more people from diverse audiences wanted to watch because they were represented in them? A recent study of the US film industry concluded that it is not only our least diverse business sector but that the exclusion of Black creators, producers, directors, and writers has cost Hollywood $10 billion annually. Films with two or more Black people in these critical behind-the-camera roles have a 10 percent higher return on investment than those with none.[4] And consider that *Barbie*, a comedy-fantasy about being female, helmed by a female director, became one of the highest-grossing films of all time within three weeks of opening in 2023, making $1 billion at the box office.[5]

Companies make many products that are intended for everyone yet do not reach their potential because they do not consider the experience that all people have when choosing and using them. They also make products for specific market segments that can have broader appeal. Consider a classic example: how people without physical disabilities benefit from accommodations designed for people who have them. If you have used an automatic door when your arms are full of packages, or turned closed-captioned programming on and the volume off when watching TV so you don't disturb your napping partner, your life is also better for the focused attention on consumers who use wheelchairs or have impaired hearing.

Organizations that offer services have similar opportunities. A survey of over 450 financial professionals by Fidelity Investments found that respondents at diversity-focused firms were more likely than other firms to say they had the right people to serve and connect with the next generation of clients and were more likely to have added clients in the previous year.[6]

Research like this has spawned innovation, including in the form of boutique investment firms like Ellevest. It has also spurred established firms to rethink how they offer financial advice. At seventy-five-year-old Fidelity, CEO Abigail Johnson and her executive team increased their efforts to create a more diverse workforce and management team.[7] They also incorporated into the investment advising process what they learned about how members of their younger, more diverse customer base make decisions.[8]

Or consider the changes that Cartier has made to how it markets and sells its exquisite jewelry and watches, most of which are designed for women. For much of its 176-year history, these luxury items have been marketed to men as gifts for the women in their lives. In the decades since women have entered the workforce in large numbers, despite gaining their own disposable income, high-end jewelry remained something "that was saved for romance, that somebody else was going to give to you," observes Mercedes Abramo, deputy chief commercial officer with Cartier International and the first woman in this role.[9] Not anymore. "We've had to pivot in the last ten years as an industry to understand that there's a whole new demographic coming up," she continues. "Many more women are obviously making those purchasing decisions." Potential customers—anyone with a lot of disposable income—are more racially and ethnically diverse, and include same-sex couples, too.

Even if women don't make the final purchase, they often do the research themselves to decide what they want (such as when choosing an engagement ring). But women are also now more likely to open their own wallets. A 2018 market research survey reported by the website *National Jeweler* found that 51 percent of women between the ages of twenty-five and forty with household incomes of $75,000 or more purchased their own jewelry. Asked about their preferences, respondents favored diamonds, other gemstones, and platinum with diamonds as their top choices.[10]

Cartier asks itself what women want to buy, not just what men want to buy for them. We all know that people choose differently when they are giving a gift than when choosing for themselves. You may not always sell the same bracelet or earrings to a man buying a gift for his mother or partner as you would to the woman who is going to wear it. The sales representatives sell differently, too. "We have worked with our sales teams on encouraging the female to have a voice in the decision-making," Abramo says. "You got that promotion; this would be a great way to commemorate that for yourself. Approaching every person walking in the door as if they themselves could be a client."[11]

If you supply other businesses rather than sell to consumers, having a more diverse leadership team matters to your clients, too. In the past, legal requirements or reputational considerations often motivated companies to engage diverse suppliers.[12] They might have checked their supplier diversity box by hiring companies that provide ancillary services, like cleaning, landscaping, or catering, and not have put much thought into how supplier diversity affected how they served their own customers. However, racial unrest in the United States has drawn attention to systemic discrimination against non-White people, while business leaders increasingly recognize the demographic trends that are transforming their customer base.

The University of Chicago educates students from around the world. It also serves the local South Side community through its cultural offerings, health care facilities, and support for public safety and education. But a piece was missing. The university could do even more for the community by helping build wealth, observed John Rogers, chairman and co-CEO of Ariel Investments and vice-chairman of the University of Chicago Board of Trustees. "We fall into this trap of the term *supplier diversity*, and have gotten trapped in the lowest margins, least economically viable parts of our economy. And it's something that we have to transform if we want to be able to create multigenerational wealth and opportunity for our communities," he says.[13] He calls on companies and "anchor institutions—our local hospitals and universities and museums and foundations" to commit to doing business with minority-owned professional services firms. In 2009, with Rogers's support, the university launched an annual symposium for founders of minority- and women-owned professional services firms to network with business leaders at the university. The effort has led to contracts with over ninety minority- and women-owned firms, including legal, money management, and staffing services.[14]

Beyond what you sell, the decisions you make about your stores and websites, your sales process, and your customer service will benefit from the input of more diverse voices to create an experience that engages a richly diverse population. It is not a coincidence that Rogers, the University of Chicago vice-chairman, is Black; that Abramo, the Cartier executive, is female; or that Boyd, the philanthropy advisor, who is White, has traveled the world extensively. They each bring their experiences in the world to the table when deciding how to meet the needs of the people they serve.

Igniting Innovation

Innovation taps underinvested markets, creates new ones, and makes existing products and services better. It's critical to economic growth, which makes it a top priority for CEOs and for any manager with a role in product design and development. For mission-driven organizations such as nonprofits, innovation is essential to extend their reach to stakeholders. And yet our affinity for people like us influences the ideas we pursue. Many leaders and managers are ignorant of ideas that spring from the perspectives of people who have different experiences, preferences, and needs than people in the group they belong to. They forget that innovation comes from unexpected sources.

We are more likely to trust information that comes from people we know, or who have had similar experiences, or who have certain training, skills, and credentials that we associate with experts (even though our judgments can be inaccurate).[15] Our assumptions about who has good ideas, who will be a good leader, and who will be a good "fit" for a role are influenced by a combination of what we have been told, what we have observed, what we have experienced, how the system was built by those who came before us, and what our colleagues think. In fact, it matters whether a colleague vouches for someone who differs from us.[16]

Many leaders and managers are ignorant of ideas that spring from the perspectives of people who have different experiences, preferences, and needs than people in the group they belong to. They forget that innovation comes from unexpected sources.

Here is a story about entrepreneur Star Cunningham to show you what I'm talking about. Before launching 4D Healthware, an online service to help patients with chronic illnesses manage their treatment and communicate with doctors, Cunningham traveled the world for IBM. She was a highly compensated consultant and industry expert with an MBA from a top business school. She managed deals worth up to $1 billion for the company's largest customers in the telecommunications sector, developed new products, and advised the C-suite on corporate strategy.[17] Moreover, she had plenty of experience as a patient with chronic illnesses managing her health care with multiple providers, and she had identified a solution to an acknowledged problem. Yet it took her five years to raise her first round of seed capital—longer than most companies at the time.[18] As of 2021 the private company, which does not report its revenues, had raised a reported $5.5 million from investors.[19]

Cunningham is a Black woman without a medical degree, and she attributes the reluctance of potential investors (White men) and customers (doctors) to her not looking like a health care entrepreneur to many of them.[20] But research in health care has shown that when patients are involved more directly in the management of their conditions, they become healthier and less likely to require expensive hospital care.[21] Millions of Americans have diabetes and heart disease, and Blacks are more likely than most other Americans to die from them.[22] "It takes somebody that knows consumers, and software, and design" to create a solution that patients will want to use, Cunningham says. "My experience belongs in the room."[23]

Her company got its first major boost in 2016 from Esther Dyson, an influential technology analyst, author, entrepreneur, and former journalist who invests her considerable fortune in a few industries, including health care. Dyson looks for investments "in people who want to solve a problem, not just sell a product or embellish their own CV," and in projects that she can learn from.[24] When Cunningham pitched her company to Dyson, they found common ground.

Critically, Dyson provides more than money. Cunningham considers her a mentor—and a bridge to other investors. "She's able to help them understand: This is what I'm gonna do, I advise you to do something similar."[25] Dyson sees what other investors do not because she looks for opportunities differently: she is interested in the potential to deliver value beyond a financial return. When she shares her perspective, she helps people who are not like her see value that was invisible to them because it didn't look the way they expected.

I have sat in countless meetings and observed the same three to five people dominate the discussion and decision-making. If the ideas that get the green light in your organization tend to come from one group, and people from the same group choose them, your process for generating and vetting ideas bears close examination.

When our colleagues are more diverse, we innovate more successfully.[26] Here's another example of what happens when you peer below the surface to look at problems from the perspectives of people who differ from you. After P&G bought Gillette, the razor manufacturer, in 2005, "we discovered we were inherently unsuccessful in India," former chairman and CEO Robert McDonald told me.[27] To understand why, he asked how Gillette had researched the market. The company, which is based in Boston, had hired some students from India attending the Massachusetts Institute of Technology, a few miles away, to test its razors. But McDonald knew the experience of shaving in the United States wasn't the same as it would be in India, where many people do not have regular access to running water. "I knew this because I had lived in the Philippines," he says, where running water was also not consistently available. "And men would sit on the floor of their dwelling and use an old fruit can of water to shave, which means they're not able to rinse. Whereas the guys at MIT are rinsing their razor under running water. I sent the team to India. They invented a new razor, and that razor did very well."

Though McDonald is a White man, he had lived and worked in a place that gave him relevant insight into the problem that needed to be solved. But you don't need a CEO to tell you where to find insights that differ from yours. Every manager has direct access to these insights through the people working in their organizations, even if they are on a different team, based in a different office, or living in another region or country.

They may have been raised on farms or in cities, traveled the world as children with their military or diplomat parents, or never left the region where they were born. Engineers, writers, factory-floor workers, frontline salespeople, people who speak multiple languages, first-generation college students, people whose parents have PhDs: they all have different ways of looking at problems. When you include them, you include the experiences that shape their worldviews. And you will see more opportunities to serve millions of people in our diverse world.

Responding to Business Change

In every era, business leaders have grappled with trends and crises that arise from technological advances, shifting market dynamics, natural disasters, and economic downturns. The more imminent the threat, the swifter and more wrenching the change is likely to be. When forced by a crisis, such as the COVID-19 pandemic, or the expected economic disruption from artificial intelligence, the stakes are especially high.

Boston Consulting Group found that after a serious financial crisis, fresh thinking, whether from a new CEO, a new leadership team, or both, was a significant factor in companies' long-term success.[28] Great ideas aren't enough, however. A business transformation or turnaround requires leaders who can inspire followers along a new and challenging path.

We should be concerned about appointing the right individuals as leaders. But it's also crucial to think about our leadership and management teams collectively being able to steer an organization through change, because change is constant. A crisis that demands dynamic new leadership presents firms with a chance to make more diverse teams the default when selecting qualified executives and managers at any level.

Maria Boulden, who became an expert at transforming sales teams during her thirty-three years at DuPont, shows us how any people leader can harness diversity to enable and support change. Among its products, DuPont makes a portfolio of materials that go into photovoltaic panels that generate electricity from sunlight. In 2010, as the company emerged from the Great Recession, its sales and market share of these products had been battered. Boulden was appointed global sales director for the unit and tasked with fixing it. It was clear to her that she needed a more diverse team to reinvigorate sales. Although DuPont's customers were mainly outside the United States, "we were still very US led, US thinking, US execution."[29] She took an organization that mostly White American men had directed and delegated responsibility to sales leaders around the world who were diverse in gender, race, ethnicity, and religion. With Boulden holding them to rigorous standards, the team established new practices for working with their channel partners and developed fresh commercial insights. DuPont's market share climbed from 12 percent to over 70 percent. A year later, the team won an internal award for sales excellence.

Observe that Boulden was a middle manager. To deliver big results—rescue a struggling business—she made a deliberate choice to tap the full range of knowledge, experience, and perspectives available to her. "Sometimes institutional knowledge is a crutch or a shield, and neither are good," she says. "That same shield that you're using to say, 'Well, this is the way the business has to be,' is holding you back from realizing what it can be. Diversity of thought is what really breaks through that traditional way of this is how the business works."

In addition, people may experience change and respond to it in different ways. Our gender, race, ethnicity, religion, education, physical abilities, and the many other characteristics that make us human influence us all. How leaders communicate change can affect individuals to varying degrees and also affect what they think about it. We willingly follow leaders who we believe understand our experiences and aspirations, and who show us they can deliver. We are more likely to leave an organization when we feel no one values our hopes or concerns. Having greater diversity in leadership and management becomes an important tool for retention. When you understand the changes that your business faces and how they affect people, you will see opportunities to build leadership and management teams that each employee feels some affinity to. Individuals may feel connected to a leader because of experiences they share, how they lead, or both.

Building and Maintaining a Good Corporate Reputation

It's hard to find an organization that doesn't care about its reputation and the forces that influence it. And with good reason. Reputation correlates with financial success. One study found that firms with superior reputations were less likely to go bankrupt.[30] Meanwhile, people around the world consistently tell pollsters and other researchers that whether they trust a brand affects what they choose to buy and where they choose to work. It's not enough to produce good-quality, reliable products and services. It also matters that an organization is a good employer, and, increasingly, that it upholds values that matter to its stakeholders and contributes to society.

Reputation and trust are two sides of a coin. As research from Edelman, the public relations firm, notes, reputation is determined by what you have done in the past, while trust predicts whether stakeholders will support you in the future.[31] More diverse teams help companies build and maintain good reputations by making more inclusive decisions and building greater trust with investors, employees, customers, and the public at large. To an extent, given rising expectations that leaders represent the full range of humanity, the diversity in your leadership and management teams is itself a reputation test.

It's easy to find examples of businesses turning to a woman or someone from an underrepresented group after they have damaged their reputation. For example, in 2019, Prada brought on award-winning filmmaker Ava DuVernay, a Black woman, as chair of the diversity and inclusion advisory board it created after it marketed a product line using racist imagery. However, the benefit of including more diverse leaders is not to preempt blunders, as important as that is. Organizations create positive impressions through actions they take rather than by what they avoid doing, which the public never hears about. They can use their good reputation to fuel other business objectives and make their organizations stronger.

Monsanto offers an example. When it was acquired by Bayer in 2018, it held the dubious distinction of being the world's most hated company due to a history replete with controversies. It had manufactured Agent Orange, a defoliant used during the Vietnam War, and it was involved in production of genetically modified (GMO) foods. Top executives wanted to confront and begin to change that reputation. Appointing racially and ethnically diverse women to senior leadership roles had a significant, positive impact on this effort.

In the first decade of the twenty-first century, the company had taken hits from anti-GMO activists, and by 2013, it had dropped efforts to sell genetically modified foods in Europe.[32] Executives concluded they had done a poor job of communicating with the public about GMOs; in fact, they had barely participated in the dialogue. When the company did weigh in, it highlighted its own research about food safety and the benefits it saw for farmers. But consumers had little if any exposure to agriculture, chemistry, or genetics—and they thought negatively about Monsanto to begin with. They didn't think the crops were safe to eat. And those consumers, through their decisions about what food to buy and their political influence, were determining which products Monsanto could sell, and where.

The company commissioned a study to learn who was influencing its poor reputation. We learned that millennial, food-minded, and female consumers, and particularly mothers, did not trust Monsanto and its top leaders, all but one of whom were male. While no set of leaders could turn around such a deeply tarnished reputation quickly, having executives who consumers believed understood their concerns would provide a foundation for building greater trust—and improving the company's reputation. The data helped me to argue that having more female leaders would help Monsanto communicate more effectively with female consumers.

Monsanto needed more leaders, period, to achieve its growth plans, and the company had already committed to developing its in-house talent. Executives understood they could meet their future leadership needs by investing in people they had unintentionally overlooked. So I worked with them to ensure we identified women who were ready for bigger roles. We promoted women into five senior leadership roles globally over two years.

The women included Shilpa Divekar Nirula, who became managing director and CEO for the India business. She was ready to assume this role based on her tenure as the second-ranking executive in the unit. But top executives also considered the benefits of having a woman as the face of the company in a country where 90 percent of the influencers of the brand reputation were women.

Another was Brazil-born Leticia Gonçalves, who became head of the Europe, Middle East, and Africa division. During her four-year tenure, Gonçalves's team tracked how the company was described in articles and social media. Over time, she told me, portrayals of Monsanto shifted, becoming less negative. Gonçalves attributes these results in part to how she identified herself to journalists and other influencers as a woman and a mother. "I spent time for them to get to know me before I positioned myself as the spokesperson," she says.[33] "I think there is more appetite to trust women versus [being] associated with the company in a bad way. So in many cases part of the conversation was talking about family, talking about who I am, and my values." If influencers could relate to her, they might be more willing to listen to her. It didn't always work, she says, "but in many cases, I could help their perceptions and their trust of the company by allowing people to get to know me."

Notice that to learn whose opinions were important to Monsanto, we looked beyond the obvious stakeholders—customers and employees. The future of your team, department, region, or organization also depends on people who do not have direct experience with your organization, such as potential customers, clients, employees, and the public. The investors, partners, suppliers, political leaders, and regulators who decide whether you can do business at all also matter. Groups that have no business with your organization may have more influence than those who do. You ignore them at your peril.

Managing Risk and Making Smarter Bets

Researchers made headlines a few years ago with a study that found women were more likely to die of a heart attack in the emergency room when they were treated by a male physician than by a female physician. They also discovered that having a higher percentage of female doctors on the ward increased women's chances of survival even when their doctor was a man. When male doctors had regular exposure to the perspectives of female colleagues, they saved more lives.[34]

Businesspeople do not make life-or-death decisions daily the way emergency room doctors do. But they nevertheless take risks that affect whether their companies will be successful. Any time an organization pursues a new opportunity, it may fail, with consequences beyond the bottom line for employees, customers, and the communities in which they operate.

Meanwhile, we live in a volatile world, full of risks—many of them age-old—that business leaders can't control. We face labor shortages, public-health crises, natural disasters, technological change, social unrest, and war. The past few decades have brought, in addition, cyberattacks, global terrorism, large-scale industrial accidents, supply chain disruptions, and climate change.

The case for representing a more diverse range of people in leadership and management has recently gained attention, and some momentum, in part because of the evidence that doing so makes organizations more stable. This is because more diverse groups have more robust discussions. They tend to offer more information, share alternative points of view, and perform better than homogenous groups.[35]

Why? We're all human, so we're going to make mistakes, no matter who we are. None of us has access to perfect information. We can't predict the future, and we certainly don't have perfect judgment. We all make assumptions and have enthusiasms. If we surround ourselves only with people who are like us, we are less likely to know what we're missing. When we include people with different backgrounds, especially when they have perspectives that are relevant to the risks we are facing, we not only make smarter bets, but we are also less likely to make truly bad ones—the kind that lead to financial, reputational, or legal ruin.

It's hard to think of a better tale of corporate risk and ruin than the banking crisis that led to the Great Recession in 2008. Millions of people lost their homes, and hundreds of banks collapsed. Among them was the investment bank Lehman Brothers. Its bankruptcy was the largest in US history. In the aftermath, Christine Lagarde, the French finance minister, quipped to a journalist that had Lehman Brothers been called Lehman Sisters, the economic crisis would have unfolded differently.[36] The remark spawned a profusion of counterfactual speculation, fueled by the historical absence of women in senior leadership roles across the financial services industry. What if more women had been involved in deciding whether to build a business on risky loans? Could more female representation have prevented a global financial meltdown and the resultant harm to so many lives?

Obviously, we can't know the answers to these questions. But Anne Finucane, who retired in 2021 as the vice-chair of Bank of America, has observed that diversity of any kind changes the decision-making process. "I think when you have diversity, whether it's by gender or race, ethnicity, sexual—whatever the diversity is—it creates the need for engagement, because you're just not alike. So, you ask a question, and the asking of the question releases everybody else to ask the question," she says.[37]

Increasing pressure from institutional investors in public companies to diversify management boards and senior executive teams may be enough of a reason for top executives to act. Nonprofit leaders may face similar calls from donors. Even if you are not facing direct investor or donor pressure, you will need to discover how greater diversity in leadership and management will help you manage risk more effectively.

You can start by being curious about your personal blind spots and those of your teammates or colleagues. Because that's where risk hides—in our assumptions, our attitudes, the questions we don't ask. Your blind spots may insulate you from diverse points of view that illuminate not only risks but also whether it is smart to take them and how you can mitigate them.

Consider the resources that go into a merger: not only money, but time and energy. A corporate board member I know recalled a merger decision that a fellow board member questioned, but which proceeded because many other board members had a relationship with the target organization. Ultimately, they had to unwind the merger, at an additional cost to everyone involved: time, money, and energy again, plus the hit to both companies' reputations.

Decision-makers can also be so risk averse that they ignore chances they need to take—including pursuing innovations that are necessary for the business to thrive. Think about Kodak, which filed for bankruptcy in 2012. Kodak engineers invented the digital camera, but its corporate culture discouraged dissent. Its leadership prioritized protecting its legacy products over exploring new business models. Fifty years ago, Kodak ranked near the top of the Fortune 500, with profits equivalent to nearly $3 billion today. But the company that invented the "Kodak moment"—a scene so memorable it had to be captured on film—fell because of its inability to capitalize on digital photography. It failed to anticipate or respond quickly enough to the threats that smartphones and online photo sharing posed to one of its core businesses: selling cameras, film, and photo paper to consumers. When it emerged from bankruptcy, it abandoned the consumer market entirely.[38]

It isn't necessary, or usually even feasible, to align the need for a more diverse set of leaders with all your organization's business priorities at once. Home in on one or two that are most urgent for the entire organization, if you are a C-level or functional leader, or for your team, if you are a middle manager. What leaders do you need? That will depend on what you learn about whose voices are missing when you are making decisions, and what you are missing by not including them as leaders and managers. When you have some answers, you will be ready for the next stage in the framework: building strong partnerships with stakeholders.

Questions for Aligning Diversity, Equity, and Inclusion with Business Priorities

The questions I suggest below aren't exhaustive. They are a way to start building an understanding of how people who differ from the majority in your organization have been hidden, and to prompt you to keep asking questions.

Creating Better Customer Experiences

- Who buys our products and services? Who does not?
- Who will our customers be in the future?
- What are the experiences of customers in different segments when using our products and services or when interacting with our organization?
- When we engage with colleagues, customers, or other stakeholders, do we talk about what we want more than we listen to what they need?

Igniting Innovation

- Whose problems do we see? Have we asked our customers in different segments what problems they're trying to solve?
- When we consider any problem, do we assume there is only one way to interpret or approach it?
- Do our processes for generating and vetting ideas include people who are closest to the problem?
- Who gets the green light? Do the ideas we pursue tend to come from the same group of people?

Responding to Business Change

- What changes are facing our business?
- Who is affected by these changes?
- Whose views have we sought about where the organization is going and how to get there? Whom haven't we asked?
- Have we considered how the decisions we are making affect diverse stakeholder groups?

Building and Maintaining a Good Corporate Reputation

- Whose opinions are important to our organization's ability to earn revenue, attract and retain employees, and maintain its license to operate?
- What matters to these influencers?
- Have we focused on what we want from our stakeholders versus what we want for them?
- Who is responsible for keeping our stakeholders satisfied?

Managing Risk and Making Smarter Bets

- Who gets invited to a meeting—any meeting? Are we including the people who are closest to the work and giving them the opportunity to ask questions and share their opinions?

- Do we make it a habit to invite people to disagree and debate with us and with each other respectfully?

- If our team is looking for new businesses to buy, whom do we turn to for help? Are there places we are not looking?

- Are smart risks rewarded? Do we celebrate people who try new and better ways of doing things, regardless of the outcome?

3 Pillar B: How to Build Strong Partnerships with Stakeholders

You won't get far without partners. When you understand what is driving your organization and what it wants to achieve (pillar A), you can start to identify the people who have a stake in addressing diversity, equity, and inclusion in leadership and management. By joining with them, whoever and wherever they are, you can enlist their influence to build support and prompt action.

This is the purpose of pillar B: build strong partnerships with stakeholders. This chapter will show you how to create a network of colleagues with the influence and expertise you need to achieve your goals, and a way to get attention for them. The good news is that partners can come from anywhere. They can include anyone who cares about having more diversity in leadership and management, as this story from Codie Sanchez shows.

Sanchez is a small business entrepreneur, and she thinks like I do. She will tell you that the secret to her success is contrarian thinking (also the name of her company, which advises people how to be financially independent by owning small businesses). In a nutshell, she means she finds opportunities to make money by being curious and asking lots of questions—a trait she developed as an undergraduate journalism major. The answers lead to insights that she wouldn't have if she simply took for granted what everyone else believes or thinks they know. And she can discover opportunities before too many other people do, because they don't know what she does.

She told me about a gathering of entrepreneurs she knows. During the conversation, one man confessed he struggled to hire women for his startup advertising agency. "We have this kind of bro culture. We were a bunch of young guys when we started [the agency], and it's been pervasive actually," Sanchez recalls him saying.[1] The firm hired a female executive once. She sued them, and they settled. But the man, nervous about repeating the experience, became afraid to hire more women.

Two women in the group were quick to judge him, and Sanchez was tempted as well. But her training kicked in; she asked him questions instead. How successful was the agency at winning accounts with companies run by women? And how much of the company's business did they represent? It turned out that the agency, which specialized in health and beauty products, was pitching mainly to woman-owned firms, and they weren't getting the business.

> And I said, "So, how could you sell to a group of humans that you don't represent at all? You have two options. Your option is to play in the man-space forever and watch your market share dwindle. Or deal with some of this cultural issue that you have. Find a way to have a fun, edgy, quirky, you-don't-have-to-be-politically-correct-all-the-time environment, but make women feel safe and comfortable inside of it. It's not going to be easy, but it's either that or a dwindling market. You gotta pick between the two, I think."

Her questions—and her conclusion—instantly reframed his issues with hiring women from a problem to be avoided to an opportunity to be embraced. Her friend—she knows him well, and she likes and respects him—hadn't considered what his company was giving up by leaving women out.

Sanchez could influence her friend because she motivated and encouraged him to fix the environment. She conveyed that his task, though it seemed daunting, was worthwhile, and that he could succeed if he tackled it. He listened to her because they had a trusting relationship as friends and fellow business leaders who helped each other solve problems. When you are building your own relationships, you will want to find the Codie Sanchezes in your organization and in your wider network: people who will act and will prompt others to do so because they can see that it is in the organization's interest—and possibly in their personal interest as well.

You may have people in your organization, even on your team, who employees consider influencers and role models, even if they do not have a prominent or formal leadership role. These may be the leaders and managers whose teams employees want to join, people they seek as mentors and coaches, or anyone they admire for any reason. (And if you see yourself in this description, embrace your role as an influencer and find the people who need your help.) People who care about diversity, equity, and inclusion will want to join you if they know you share their interest, even if their reasons differ from yours.

Whom you enlist in your efforts, and how you gain their support, will depend on your role, the people you have access to, and how your aims for greater leadership diversity align with your business objectives. A CEO will turn to their direct reports, the board, and shareholders. A diversity, equity, and inclusion leader will enlist the CEO, their boss, leaders and managers at all levels, influential employees, and the internal HR community. A middle manager has their boss, their team members, their colleagues, their HR partners (including the diversity, equity, and inclusion leader), and, if their role is externally facing, their customers or suppliers.

Everyone will tailor their list to their situation. But whoever they are, stakeholders have many reasons to become partners. These may be

Financial: They understand, or can be shown, that the organization, their business units, or their investments will be more profitable when teams that are representative of their workforce and customers are making decisions.

Operational: Businesses need people to run them, and the competition for leadership talent is fierce. They understand, or can be shown, that it will be harder for their organizations to find the best people for leadership and management roles unless they include people from relevant demographic groups. It's a simple case of supply and demand.

Personal: A personal stake can inspire people. They may relate these to achieving their performance goals, their career aspirations, or their core beliefs. A belief in fairness and equality can motivate people, at least in part.

Of course, people can have more than one stake. Part of building strong partnerships is uncovering where someone's interests lie, which of their interests is most important to them, and the barriers to them acting. Set aside your assumptions about them and ask questions that get them talking about their vision (if they have one) for and their experiences (or lack of them) with diversity, equity, and inclusion. Only when you know a person can you deliver what they need to support you and do what you need them to do. This is true whether you are a department head choosing staff for a project or a diversity, equity, and inclusion leader coaching senior executives to create an inclusive process for mentoring high-potential talent.

For example, Mark Mendez is a partner at the law firm Davis Polk, where he heads the derivatives and structured products group. He has been responsible for assigning associates to work with partners on transactions, which means it has been his job to equitably distribute opportunities to gain experience. "Some transactions are better to work on than others because of the clients you get to work with, the learning opportunities, the partner you get to work with, how high-profile the transaction is within the firm," Mendez says.[2] "A partner calls and says, 'Can I work with person X, Y, Z?' There is some push and pull in terms of trying to explain to my partners why it might be more equitable to have this person work on a high-profile transaction because she didn't get to work on the last such transaction." He has advised partners to spend more time with associates "explaining the background, explaining the legal issue, explaining the particular challenges of this client and why they're hard to work with. . . . Some of the things that you take for granted but that might make the experience more rewarding."

In all organizations, leaders choose which team members get which opportunities. They collaborate with project leaders or department heads who may have their own ideas about who should have an assignment. Mendez supports his stakeholders by sharing the reasons behind his recommendations and offering partners advice for building successful relationships with team members they may not have worked with previously.

As this story illustrates, your stakeholders may not know that they need to develop a more diverse set of leaders or be ready to do something about it. It may be easy to persuade them once you identify their motivations and offer them help. However, some stakeholders may not agree with all of your goals, or your approach, or they may have other priorities that are more important to them. You will still need them in your coalition, though it may take more time, effort, and help from other influencers to engage them.

Stakeholders Are Everywhere

Everyone is a stakeholder for someone. The board of directors, CEO, and other members of the C-suite are stakeholders because they set the agenda for the whole organization. The next level of leaders—who may include functional and line-of-business executives—are stakeholders because they carry out that agenda. Middle managers are stakeholders because they are advocates for their high-potential employees. Often they do not feel empowered to push for greater diversity, equity, and inclusion at higher levels in the organization. Nevertheless, good managers want to see their talented employees thrive and may become strong proponents of their advancement. Employees are stakeholders, too, because they care about their jobs and their futures. And many managers have a tool—employee surveys—that, if they segment demographic data, they can use to learn who is happy, who is engaged (or not), what they think about their career opportunities, and whether they feel supported by their colleagues and supervisors.

Managers can engage employees on their teams as individual stakeholders. They can also involve them through formal and informal employee groups that mobilize around initiatives to improve the work environment. These groups may have power and influence through their relationships with other stakeholders. For instance, customers, partners, and suppliers may trust frontline employees more than management. The groups can be a conduit for what these stakeholders think about the need for diversity, equity, and inclusion in the business broadly. In one company, I partnered these groups with our business development team. They acted as cultural attachés for customers visiting from countries where English is not the primary language. This collaboration led to the first purchase of one of our products by a customer in China.

Employees may organize around any issue that is important to them. If they own company stock, they may even propose shareholder resolutions, as Amazon employees did in 2018, asking the company to reduce its fossil fuel emissions. Although the resolution lost, it galvanized employees. Pressure from them influenced then CEO Jeff Bezos to commit to reducing Amazon's carbon footprint, in part by purchasing electric delivery trucks and converting to 100 percent renewable energy by 2030.[3] Some of the most influential employees may even be the ones who walk out the door. You can turn their rejection of the organization into a cause for action.

Influence comes from outside the organization, too. If your role allows, you can partner with external stakeholders such as investors, donors, and customers who exert good old-fashioned pressure. They will vote with their shareholder proxies and their wallets.

Prominent shareholders have, for instance, begun to push for greater diversity among directors on corporate boards and in top management.

Their advocacy may come with advice, resources, and relationships that help the organization move forward. In 2019 activist investor Arjuna Capital, led by managing director Natasha Lamb, introduced a shareholder resolution to Citi that pushed the company to publish its pay data. The data revealed that pay for women was 29 percent less than for men, and 7 percent less for racial minorities due to their underrepresentation in top positions. (Other data from Citi showed that women and men in the same jobs were paid about the same.) Citi's head of human resources told the *Washington Post* that the firm aimed "to be as transparent as possible to employees about why representation matters."[4] Citi set goals for increasing representation in middle management roles for women globally and Blacks in the United States. By targeting middle management—from assistant vice presidents to managing directors—Citi has taken steps to develop its bench of leaders from these groups.

When external influencers like Natasha Lamb can capture the attention of board members and senior executives, they create openings for change. It is unlikely to have been news to anyone at Citi that their leadership teams underrepresented racial and ethnic minorities or women, even if they had not thought about the extent of the gaps or the reasons for them.

But external stakeholders, including investors and policymakers, have also pushed back against diversity, equity, and inclusion. We can understand where they are coming from by engaging with and listening to them, just as we do other stakeholders. Listening doesn't imply that we agree with them or commit us to doing what they want. It's an invitation to dialogue that gives us information we need to continue making progress. As we learned at Monsanto, avoiding these challenges won't make them go away.

The more stakeholders that diversity, equity, and inclusion advocates have, in many positions of influence within and outside their organizations, the more levers they can pull and the more action they will generate.

The World of Stakeholders at Rockwell Collins

The following story about Rockwell Collins will help you see the range of people who had a stake and a role in diversity, equity, and inclusion and how we supported each other. Later in this chapter, I will show you how to identify and engage your stakeholders wherever you sit in your organization.

From 2006 to 2009 I served as the global chief diversity and inclusion officer at Rockwell Collins (which has since been acquired by Raytheon Technologies). When I started, the company was beginning to hire seven thousand engineers in five years. It was easy to see that we could not meet our hiring goals without recruiting from a more diverse talent pool outside of the Midwest. Executives did not need convincing. However, our industry—aerospace—was male dominated and the population in our location—Cedar Rapids, Iowa—was overwhelmingly White. Recruiting and retaining women and non-White employees had always been challenging, and I knew we would need help from inside and outside the company. I almost didn't take the job myself.

Here are some stakeholders I engaged with besides the executive team: community relations, recruiting, university relations, leadership development, marketing, communications, government relations, Rockwell Collins's Chief Engineering Council, and, of course, the middle managers who had an urgent need for talent. Together, we created partnerships with universities and professional associations where our leaders and managers could meet faculty, students, and professionals with a wider range of backgrounds and experiences. They could communicate our growing need for talent; our efforts to build a team that encompassed women, racial and ethnic minorities, and people with physical disabilities and other differences; and our work to create an inclusive professional environment.

These partnerships helped to achieve another purpose as well: to develop future leaders. Rockwell Collins's senior executives cared deeply about developing leaders internally. Having masterful communications skills and an ability to build powerful networks were critical to advancing in the leadership ranks. I worked with our leadership development teams to get speaking engagements for these rising leaders and managers and to place them in advisory roles with organizations that served a broad array of populations. These opportunities helped them gain visibility and hone their communications skills. We also paved the way for recruitment by raising the profile of the company and its commitment to diversity, equity, and inclusion while interacting with the diverse set of people whose talent we needed.

My role enabled me to negotiate a spot for the company's only female executive on an advisory board at the Georgia Institute of Technology, a public university with one of the strongest undergraduate engineering programs in the United States and a racially and ethnically diverse student body. As the senior vice president for engineering and technology, she had essential knowledge about the industry and the company culture to share with the university. She could also influence the curriculum in ways that benefited the industry. This executive became a champion for the university, facilitating intimate meetings among faculty, students, and key company stakeholders, including our CEO, on a range of topics.

Because of this strategic partnership with Georgia Tech, we hired more engineers from there than we had previously. We also created internships for students and fellowships for faculty. When they returned to campus, they became ambassadors for the company. Meanwhile, the insight we gained from these relationships—and from academia overall—enabled us to create a more inclusive workplace. And the exposure that the senior vice president received helped her extend her network and grow as a leader.

I also provided tangible support for middle managers in their day-to-day work. All our efforts to recruit new hires would have come to nothing if we did not deliver the people they needed or if those people did not stay. Some issues managers faced were systemic; alleviating their frustrations would make their jobs as team leaders easier. One step was to make it easier to bring new hires on board, beginning with the offer process. We knew that most of our recruits would relocate from another part of the country, and that their partners, if they had them, would be part of the decision. So we helped the partners find jobs (within or outside the company), if possible, or volunteer opportunities. We also worked with our HR partners, facilities, and IT to make it easier for managers to get space and equipment for new hires once they agreed to work for us—a process that had long frustrated both parties.

I mentioned that the company had difficulty retaining female and non-White engineers. We needed to work harder at that, too. So we gave managers more ways to learn how employees felt about their jobs and the work environment. For example, my team partnered with HR to survey new hires after thirty, sixty, and a hundred days to learn about their interviewing and onboarding experience, how they were becoming integrated with their teams, how they were connecting with managers, and how they viewed the community. We fed that information back to managers with advice about how to address concerns that employees identified.

The changes we set in motion cascaded through the Cedar Rapids and nearby Iowa City communities. Many of our young, ethnically diverse new employees provided valuable advice about how to make these cities more welcoming and inclusive (which we understood was important to keeping them). They influenced one local bank to change its advertising and messaging, which had targeted White people over fifty, to feature people who were ethnically diverse and younger. The bank understood these residents had disposable income, and it wanted them as customers—another example of a business objective that benefited from attention to diversity, equity, and inclusion.

Consider all the stakeholders in this story and their relationships. First, our executive team, which was staking the company on its ability to attract engineering talent. Next, the leaders who were in charge of the corporate image, as well as creating and maintaining good relationships with our many external communities—where we operated, where we recruited talent, where we exchanged ideas and shaped the future of our technology-driven industry. Also, middle managers who could not meet their business and performance objectives without recruiting and retaining more talent, and who gained opportunities to develop their skills. The diverse employees we hired, meanwhile, had a stake in making Cedar Rapids and Iowa City places that would welcome them. In every organization, including yours, people have the same interests.

As this story also shows, every organization has many external stakeholders. For Rockwell Collins, these included universities across the country, which were motivated to expand employment opportunities for their graduates and to collaborate on innovation, as well as local businesses, which benefited from the influx of young people with money to spend. It helped that Rockwell Collins's leadership, including the board of directors, and the larger business community were open-minded and welcoming. Combine a progressive attitude with a business need for talent, and it isn't as hard to get people to change the way they think about diversity, equity, and inclusion, or to act. Community leaders, including the mayor, along with local retailers, home builders, health care providers, real estate and arts and culture leaders all joined our efforts.

Stakeholders Are People, Not Boxes on an Organizational Chart

When you have identified the roles where you will find your stakeholders, and you have some ideas about why people in these roles will, or should, want to help you, you can find the specific people you need to engage. This will be an ongoing process, for two reasons. First, your business, and its progress toward building more diverse leadership and management teams, will evolve. And second, individuals will change roles, business goals will change, and each stage of your efforts may require help from different influencers. This is true of building and maintaining support for any business initiative.

It's critical, therefore, to remember that you are building relationships with people, not boxes on an organizational chart. Only when you understand who a person is can you truly understand what you need to do to convince them to act. Our humanity matters profoundly—so much, in fact, that according to research by sociologist Joseph Grenny and colleagues, getting people to behave differently has nothing specifically to do with evidence. Rather, they have to be motivated, encouraged, able to do what they are asked, and supported by both the people around them and the work environment.[5]

Helping people find their motivation, encouraging their contributions, showing them what they need to do differently, and giving them what they need to succeed are skills that many effective people leaders already have and use daily. In fact, it may come to you so naturally that you don't realize you're doing it. It's much easier, however, to figure out a person who is like you: you are like fishes in a school, swimming in the same water. It takes more effort to understand what motivates someone who differs from you.

Mercedes Abramo, the deputy chief commercial officer with Cartier International, describes understanding "the 360 about the person and how we can support them" as an important tenet of her leadership.[6] "Someone early on gave me feedback that I seemed to understand what makes people tick," she recounts. "I have a sense around their motivation. Or if I don't, I try to figure out what it is. Because in trying to get to a solution or partner with somebody if they're on the opposite end of the spectrum on a topic I want to understand why."

Similarly, I approach every encounter as an opportunity to build my awareness about a person: to acknowledge and accept what I don't know or understand about them or their point of view and to keep asking questions so that I do. Starting with a clean slate, as I gain information, my partner and I build rapport—and trust.

Anyone can do the same. For several years I worked with a CEO who struggled to show his commitment to increasing representation of women and racial and ethnic minorities in the leadership of his company. He sincerely believed in the goal, and he was keen to sponsor individuals. But he did not speak to groups about either his personal efforts or those of the company. I was puzzled because I knew that employees, middle managers, and even his C-suite colleagues would not fully embrace our agenda or trust that we were serious unless the CEO was a visible advocate for it. He had to show his commitment by showing up, talking about what he was doing, sharing his hopes and expectations, answering questions, and receiving feedback.

Because of the relationship that I had developed with him through one-on-one monthly meetings (where I provided updates, made requests, and served as his confidante), I eventually learned the reason. He could not sincerely talk about inclusion because he had never experienced being excluded. While he had worked very hard to achieve his position, every door had opened for him throughout his schooling and his career because of the family he was born into. Thus he could not imagine what the workplace or life was like for someone without his advantages. He had a huge blind spot. Once I learned this, I could be a better coach and advisor to him because I had a deeper awareness of his experience, strengths, and needs. But I am certain that he never would have revealed his limitation if I had not shown him my curiosity, empathy, and compassion previously, or if I had judged him for expressing his thoughts and feelings.

I had delivered a talk about the importance of diversity, equity, and inclusion, during which I taught the team about biases and assumptions and what they cost people and the business. I had also shared my findings from conversations with women around the globe about their experiences in the organization and with its leaders, and how these experiences affected their performance. Next I established a safe environment (where others would not judge their comments or discuss them outside of the group) and asked each leader to set aside their professional identities and share a story—human to human—about how they had been excluded and how that experience affected them.

The CEO chose to be the last to share, revealing his blind spot in the presence of his entire leadership team. His lack of leadership on diversity, equity, and inclusion had frustrated many of them. After this meeting, his team understood him better. We were able to create and execute a more robust diversity, equity, and inclusion strategy by adding these topics to the agenda at all company-wide meetings, creating accountability for key stakeholders, and more.

Anyone can build partnerships with their stakeholders that are as productive as those I built at Rockwell Collins and other organizations. The next section explains how.

Three Steps to Building Strong Partnerships

These steps will get you on your way:

1. Identify your stakeholders.
2. Gather intelligence.
3. Create trust by giving stakeholders what they need.

If you have experience leading people and you have helped your organization to execute a shift in direction—and diversity, equity, and inclusion is a shift for many—the three steps I outline here may sound familiar. You can still find information here that will help you apply what you know in the context of expanding diversity in leadership and management.

Identify Your Stakeholders

A good list can help you understand which stakeholders are most important to your efforts and the level of attention and assistance each of them needs. It can also help you see connections among your stakeholders that can amplify their influence.

I think about four categories of stakeholders:

People with high power and influence. These are top executives such as the board of directors, the CEO, and other C-level leaders who set the agenda for the entire organization. Big investors may also fall into this category. It's important to manage relationships with these stakeholders closely. By that I mean having regular, clear, and frank communication about diversity, equity, and inclusion goals, plans, and progress that is tailored to their roles and their individual needs. Each stakeholder in this category will have different requirements for how, when, and how often to communicate. If they are your stakeholders, they will expect you to be consistent and thorough and to deliver what you promise.

People with high power but low direct influence. These may include department heads and other middle managers who execute the decisions made by senior leaders. They make money for the business, cut its costs, achieve its mission, and control the resources for doing so. They want to be satisfied. Most importantly to any diversity, equity, and inclusion effort, middle managers decide the work that people do and manage the people who do it. Even when they support a diverse, inclusive, and equitable workplace, they need to see that the steps toward this goal consider their business needs, their people challenges, and how they will be held accountable for results.

People with lots of influence but little direct power. Stakeholders in this category can prompt action, but they do not have the power to make change directly. Many external stakeholders, including investors and important customers or suppliers, are likely to fall into this category. They want to be informed about the organization's efforts so they feel connected when you call on them for help.

People with little power or influence. These stakeholders have an interest in the outcome of your efforts, even though they play a minor role in whether they succeed or fail. Employees often fall into this category, whether they are from a dominant group or an underrepresented one. However, many employees, especially from younger generations, are not afraid to act on their interests. Knowing what they think about the work environment and their career prospects is important because their morale matters. They will want you to check in with them regularly.

A list of stakeholders can be especially useful in helping you identify and track the people or groups whose influence you need but who are not yet convinced that working toward leadership and management diversity is in their interest. They may not feel confident that they know how to make a difference, they may be afraid to have uncomfortable conversations, or they may not believe diversity, equity, and inclusion are priorities. They will need the most support while they learn what their stake is.

As you develop your list, practice getting input by asking others to point out who is missing from it. If your coalition does not include people from groups that are underrepresented in leadership, your progress will be limited. For example, if you are a leader on a team whose members are all of one race, gender, or both, your ability to understand what needs to be done to enable people who are a different race or gender is limited by your experience. You won't find the answers without acknowledging their stake in the organization and in their careers and building partnerships with them.

The same goes for the critics. People who push back against your diversity, equity, and inclusion efforts can show you the weak points that you need to address to be successful. It is possible that your approach to diversity, equity, and inclusion, the logic of your arguments, or both, are shaky. Or you may not be communicating effectively.

Patience is part of the process. You may have to dig to understand why certain stakeholders think and behave the way they do—to see their humanity—before you know whether and how you can influence them. If you can get them to join you, their positions as influencers will be powerful.

Figure 3.1
Stakeholders with varying levels of influence may come from inside and outside your organization—and may include people who are not directly involved with it.

Gather Intelligence

When you know who your stakeholders are, you can find out what matters to them, and what kind of support they need, by asking meaningful questions without judging their answers.

You have a few tools at your disposal, depending on whether you are engaging with external or internal stakeholders. Some examples include one-on-one conversations, meeting agendas, employee surveys, focus groups, and (if you have a senior role, or work with investors) shareholder resolutions.

One-on-one conversations: Talk to individual stakeholders about their experiences and perspectives. Get to know who they are beneath their roles, levels, and titles.

Your goal here is to find out what people have experienced personally in leading, managing, or working with their teams. Then you can learn what it takes for them to meet their goals and what it will take to get them to join you.

If you talk with people leaders, you can ask them why they want more diverse leaders and managers on their teams. Find out what they do to include people from underrepresented groups when evaluating employees for leadership development opportunities, filling open positions, and recommending candidates for promotion or assignments that give them exposure and a unique experience. When you talk with employees, you can ask them how they access advancement opportunities. If you lead a team, you can offer skip-level meetings to learn from people who do not report directly to you. You can also look at whether your peers are in a demographic group that is being left behind. If so, showing your support and encouragement to them individually may be all they need to gain the confidence to put themselves forward at the next opportunity.

Meeting agendas: Where you contribute to setting the agenda for any meeting about strategy, include diversity, equity, and inclusion on it.

The specific questions you discuss will vary depending on who is in the meeting, but you can use this time to learn what members understand about the business rationale for including people with a wider range of experiences and backgrounds in leadership—including whether they see one at all. You can also learn about their experiences identifying, developing, and appointing people from underrepresented groups and hear about their challenges achieving the organization's diversity, equity, and inclusion goals.

In addition, you can discuss the extent to which the leadership pipeline represents the diversity of the organization's workforce and customers, and what is being done to address any issues. As the leader of the meeting, you can nominate a few people in the room to listen and watch out for blind spots during the discussion, just as you might choose notetakers.

Employee surveys: If your organization conducts employee surveys and segments the demographic data, you can compare how employees from different groups feel about the work environment, their jobs, and their prospects for advancement.

You can use this data in a variety of ways, but it's useful for determining which groups of employees need attention, why, and where they are. Questions about whether they have development opportunities, access to or visibility with key decision-makers, and the resources they need to be productive can pinpoint areas of opportunity. Follow up with them to learn the best way to get more detailed insights and feedback. Then follow through, according to your role. Provide opportunities for them to share information and their experiences. Keep them informed, as well, of both the progress the organization is making and avenues for them to participate further. You can work with your HR and diversity, equity, and inclusion partners to respond to the findings as you do with other areas that need attention.

Focus groups: Through focus groups, customers, partners, or clients who represent different segments of your market can share how they perceive your organization, how well you serve their needs, and the value they place on diversity, equity, and inclusion. They may even have suggestions for what to do to address their concerns.

If the marketing or product teams already organize these sessions, an HR or diversity, equity, and inclusion leader can advise them on how to have more inclusive conversations with stakeholders. Leaders who are not in externally facing roles but who want to conduct their own sessions may be able to partner with them and draw on their expertise. You do not always have to ask your focus groups directly about diversity, equity, and inclusion. If you gather demographic data from any group and segment it, you can get relevant insight from any questions you ask. Similarly, members of business resource or networking groups for underrepresented employees can be sources of insight and influence. So will employees from different generations. They can tell you what they need from the organization and whether what you are doing is making a difference.

Shareholder resolutions: If you handle investor relations or communicate with the public, shareholder resolutions will help you identify the people and organizations that are trying to influence change from the outside, understand what they want, and learn how your goals and theirs align. Shareholders proposed 340 resolutions related to climate and social issues, including diversity, equity, and inclusion, in the first half of 2023, although support for them declined compared to two years earlier.[7]

Professionals in your finance and legal departments who work on shareholder issues will have information about both past trends at your shareholder meetings and upcoming proposals. You can learn about general trends by partnering with the proxy advisory firms that support institutional investors with research, data, and advice about voting their shares. With this awareness, you can have informed conversations with external stakeholders, with the potential to benefit from their expertise. Because they can compare your organization to others without being biased by internal traditions, processes, or relationships, they can offer objective assessments and advice. They may also offer help.

The purpose of all this is to learn. Whether you are a middle manager engaging with your team, the CEO meeting with business resource groups, or a director talking to investors, you're there to find out how you can be of value to that stakeholder. Conversations about race, gender, and other differences in the workplace need to be honest, and when people tell the truth about what they think and how they feel, what they say can be uncomfortable to hear. This is no different from getting feedback that your product or service does not meet a customer's expectations or being told that you and your team are not meeting your safety targets.

Uncomfortable conversations put us off balance. They engage our defenses. Senior executives have confessed to me they are afraid to talk about diversity, equity, and inclusion because they feel exposed, or they are afraid they will not measure up to what listeners expect of them. Some are aware they know next to nothing about the experiences of people who are not like themselves. And others have shared that the subject is politically explosive. Because they need to be seen as decisive and capable, and because they need to protect their people and the organization, entering a room where they may be criticized or judged for their decisions, behavior, or beliefs can be terrifying. Anyone who leads a team may feel similarly.

From the hundreds of conversations that I have had with people managers over more than two decades, it is clear that talking about issues related to identity is not easy for them, especially when they have spent most of their lives living and working with people who are very similar to themselves. But if you want strong partnerships with your stakeholders, it is crucial to be open to what they have to say, even if it takes time and effort to process it. Your goal is not to agree or disagree but to learn what you don't know. Not only that: what they tell you should prompt action. Stakeholders will not trust you, or continue to engage with you, unless you can show them you take their needs seriously. As this story from Richard Taylor, the senior vice president of people experience and diversity at Nasdaq, illustrates, your ability to listen and respond to stakeholders whether or not they are fully on board with what you are trying to do is crucial.

Taylor says he was once told by a C-level leader that White men were beginning to perceive themselves as being excluded from the company's diversity, equity, and inclusion efforts. "As a White man, this was tough to hear," he says.[8] "When I look around my organization, I see White people in positions of power everywhere." However, he continues, "I realized that the words I used and the messages I communicated were very focused on minority and marginalized communities. If all an employee hears is how we're focusing on attracting, retaining, and advancing 'diverse' people, naturally they don't see themselves in this picture and it creates a sense that 'I don't matter.'"

The answer was to feature many voices and faces in campaigns to attract talent and to understand that everyone needs to literally see representations of themselves to feel included. "And I also think this may create more allies," he concludes, "because everyone can see that everyone benefits."

Create Trust by Giving Stakeholders What They Need

If they trust you, they will trade with you. When you know what matters to your stakeholders, you can address their needs, help them meet their goals, and enable them to reciprocate with actions that contribute to your goals.

If they trust you, they will trade with you.

Recall the challenges we faced with managers at Sodexo, whose needs we initially neglected. Even when we articulated our goal, and managers' role in executing it, most were not enthusiastic about doing so, and not all believed it was necessary. However, as we recognized and addressed their needs (for explanation, education, tools, and training), they saw how they and their teams benefited. When they saw results, their opposition diminished. They began to trust the diversity, equity, and inclusion team and to seek our help.

But it wasn't enough to solve their issues once. They trusted us because we had taken the time to get to know them without judgment, put their needs first, and followed through on the commitments we made. They could rely on us when they needed advice or support. Once you establish trust, you have to reinforce it with regular communication about what you have done, what you are doing, and what you will do next. Use whatever methods you normally would to update stakeholders on the status of your initiatives. These may include any (or all) of the following, depending on your role:

- Every people leader can update their team members during one-on-one conversations (such as weekly check-ins) and regular meetings.
- Department heads, division leaders, and other executives can use formal communications, such as emails and all-hands meetings, to share information with groups of employees and managers.
- Marketing, corporate communications, or environmental, social, and governance groups can inform customers and the public through published progress reports, newsletters, or other external communications.
- Anyone who is authorized to speak with the media can take advantage of planned interviews on any topic to talk about diversity, equity, and inclusion.

Include a way for your stakeholders to tell you what they are thinking and experiencing (as we did for the executives and managers at Sodexo) so that you can continue your intelligence gathering and uncover additional needs.

As you build your partnerships with stakeholders and they use their influence, you will also build a culture of role models. The next chapter explains how.

Questions for Building Strong Partnerships with Stakeholders

The following questions will help you learn who your stakeholders are, what matters to them, and how you can motivate them to use their influence to support diversity, equity, and inclusion in your organization.

Identifying Stakeholders

- Who are they?
- What is their power in or influence on the organization?
- Who can they influence?
- What do I need them to do?

Gathering Intelligence

- Does this stakeholder think creating more diverse leadership teams is important? If so, what is motivating them? If not, ask them what could persuade them.
- What may prevent a stakeholder from using their power or influence? Do they need information, encouragement, tools, or support in order to act?
- Do I know enough about the demographic and consumer trends for my business in the next several years to identify the people who need to be my partners? How will I find out what they need?

Creating Trust

- What am I doing to show my stakeholders they can rely on me to give them what they need?
- How do I let my stakeholders know about the progress we have made and our next steps?
- How do I ensure my stakeholders can give me feedback?

4 Pillar C: How to Cultivate a Culture of Role Models

Let's be realistic: there will always be individuals who behave negatively toward people who differ from them. The question is, What should we do about it?

We are used to answering this question by punishing people when they do not comply with laws or directives that order them not to discriminate. We are less attentive to the workplace culture that acknowledges sexism, racism, homophobia, and other prejudices only when someone who has been hurt calls out a particularly egregious example. This is a significant reason we have made so little progress—why management does not represent the workplace or the population as a whole. We have not challenged and changed the systems, policies, and practices that perpetuate the status quo—intentionally or not—and routinely overlook women, people with disabilities, those who practice nondominant religions, non-White and LGBTQ+ people, or people with other differences when choosing managers and leaders.

And it is the systems, policies, and practices of an organization—how we do business, how we distribute work, how we select leaders, which results we reward—that determine the workplace culture and who is welcome in it. Whether your workplace culture is welcoming has a direct bearing on your ability to field the best possible team of leaders and managers. Pillar C of the ABCD framework provides an approach to creating a welcoming and inclusive culture wherever you sit in your organization, whether you are managing a worksite, running a department, or leading at the top. As you shift the environment, you will work closely with your stakeholders (pillar B) and connect the changes you are making to your business priorities (pillar A).

If your organization cannot create and maintain an environment that welcomes everyone, it will become difficult to retain employees from a wide range of backgrounds, who make up a growing portion of the workforce, and who it will need as leaders in the future. If you lead people (again, whether directly or indirectly), you can't defer taking on this problem: when employees are unsatisfied—especially with their managers—they will take their talent elsewhere.

However, shifting a culture is a long-term undertaking that requires role models to show what people must do differently at every step. As with any change, employees will look to their managers, and managers to the leaders above them, to understand what will make them successful. At the beginning, senior leaders will have the most impact, because they are the most visible and because they set standards of performance for the entire organization. Ultimately, however, every manager, at every level, in every office, warehouse, or factory will be a role model who represents the corporate culture through their actions.

What Is a Welcoming Culture?

If the answer to the question of what we should do is to create a welcoming culture, full of role models, the next step is to ask two questions: What does a welcoming culture look like? And how does ours compare?

Culture is the set of assumptions and practices that define social groups and determine how they interact. Systems and processes, both formal and informal, shape the culture of an organization and whether it is welcoming. Some aspects of an organization's culture can be difficult to see, or even define, because our shared assumptions are so deeply ingrained. But others are easy to identify when you look for them.

Here's one that is fundamental. If one race or gender dominates your upper and middle management teams, then the systems and policies of your organization that identify, select, and develop people as leaders and managers are, by definition, making many people from the nondominant group unwelcome. It's that simple. They are not there because of the way your business operates. It discourages them from being there, even if that is not your intent.

Consider the experiences of Kate Sullivan, an Emmy Award–winning broadcast journalist. As a reporter and anchor, Sullivan covered big stories for major markets, including New York and Chicago, before launching "To Dine For" in 2018. The program, distributed by American Public Television, features interviews by Sullivan with "creators and dreamers" over meals in their favorite restaurants.

But from the beginning, her career often hinged on criteria that had nothing to do with her talent and skills as a journalist, and that made her feel unwelcome. She recalls her first performance review:

> I remember asking, Was there anything I could do to improve my work? What I was expecting or what I had hoped to hear was, "You could make your writing sharper. You can do a better live shot. You can become more natural on camera. You can communicate with the photographer so that you bring back better material." These are all the things that I think in my mind I could have been doing better, and the answer was, "Yes, you can lose ten pounds."
>
> So, twenty-three years old, in my first job, thinking, how do I improve professionally, and that was the only thing that was said. Even this many years later, it still affects me because it wasn't just a comment from the public about they don't like my hair, or I should never wear brown, or something silly. This was from my boss. But that is one example of so many I could give you of just the reality of working in television news.[1]

Sullivan lost the weight. Meanwhile, she found mentors and colleagues—including supportive managers—who helped her develop her craft. But when she finally left television news, the culture inside the organizations where she had worked played a role. Taking nasty comments from the public is part of the job, and it can be demoralizing. More so when your managers do not have your back.

There are many reasons a person might conclude that an organization is not the right place for them. They boil down to these:

- Managers and peers devalue their contributions by focusing more on their mistakes or areas to improve than on their achievements. Meanwhile, people from the dominant group get bigger rewards—raises or bonuses—and more recognition, often for equivalent or lesser performance. Many of us can think of leaders who have behaved poorly or inappropriately yet received a promotion or a new department to lead rather than being demoted or fired.

- They are judged not according to their work but (like Sullivan) by whether their appearance, speech, or demeanor conforms to how members of the dominant group think they should look, speak, or behave.

They are frequently told that they need to change something about themselves in order to fit in.

- They do not see anyone like them in roles to which they aspire, so they lack role models to show them that achieving their ambitions is both possible and encouraged. Nor do they have access to insights or advice about navigating barriers that people with similar backgrounds and experiences have faced. They feel like no one is representing them or thinking about them, and it makes them feel lonely or invisible.

And, like Sullivan, they are hurt. By changing these practices and the behaviors that support them, you can show them you want them to participate and that you need and value their contributions. In doing so, you show your followers and your peers how to do the same.

Think about how you would welcome a group of friends to a social gathering in your home. You would arrange and manage the environment to show that you value each person's presence and their contributions to making the event enjoyable. You would acknowledge everyone. You would introduce guests who do not know each other and inform them of things they have in common to ensure that everyone has an opportunity to participate. The seating in your home would encourage people to form groups based on their interests, and also, importantly, it would not force anyone to sit alone. You would take additional steps necessary to ensure that guests felt valued and enjoyed themselves—including admonishing and, as a last resort, removing guests who were rude or disorderly. In other words, as the party host, you would orchestrate a good time by ensuring that your guests can be themselves, that they feel appreciated and respected by you and other guests, and that they are encouraged to participate in ways that make the event successful.

If you are a leader in the workplace, you are also orchestrating people—in this case, to encourage their performance and achieve your business goals. As human beings, we all have the same needs and expectations for being appreciated and valued for who we are, whether we are at a social gathering among friends or in the office among colleagues. If you invite people—your employees—to your workplace, you have no less responsibility to make them feel they belong there than when inviting friends to your house.

When Jami McKeon joined Morgan Lewis after finishing law school in 1981, she recalls female lawyers were often called "dear" and "honey," sometimes even in court, and asked if they were going to quit when they had children.[2] "But all of the partners I worked with—all of whom were men—were extremely invested in me," says McKeon, who was elected chair of the firm in 2014 and reelected twice. "If I did good work, I got more of it, and more opportunities. I immediately found the firm to be a place where I could thrive, and where I felt supported and successful right from day one." McKeon had managers who made her feel valued and who showed an interest in helping her achieve her goals. Whether an employee experiences the workplace like McKeon did is a significant factor in whether they feel an emotional connection to their organization and alignment with its goals.

Just ask David Gumbs. Gumbs is director of the RMI Islands Energy Program, which assists utilities and governments in the Caribbean with their transition to renewable energy. He joined the program, part of the Rocky Mountain Institute, after six years as the CEO of the Anguilla Electric Company, where he launched its renewable energy transformation. Corporate America "was unfamiliar territory to me like it is for most Black men in the US, right?" he says.[3] "One thing that I appreciate in American corporate culture, and American culture in general, is the very small window for acceptance, and I've always used that window to build connection to people who are different from me—and to build that connection over time," he says. "But it's really challenging. You're not your true self." Gumbs emigrated as a child, with his family, from the Caribbean to the United States and describes feeling like an outsider. "The way I spoke was different, the food I ate was different, what I liked to do for fun was different." He says he will still "turn off" his accent at times "because I need to make a specific impression."

Gumbs began his career as an accountant and financial analyst. He built relationships with colleagues, mentors, and managers who saw the value he brought to their organizations and advocated for him. But he also describes having his contributions overlooked by managers he thought were biased and concluding they were unlikely to change their minds. "I didn't sense they really appreciated me and valued me, so I moved on," he says, even when taking the risk felt difficult. "When I have a lot on the line in terms of my career growth, I'll make that decision and push through."

It wasn't until he landed at Sodexo as a director in the corporate finance department that he began to acquire the skills, experiences, and visibility he needed to become a senior executive. Sodexo was, as I noted earlier, in the process of its own culture transformation. We had created a mentorship program and forums to help employees from groups that were underrepresented in leadership make connections across the company. "I got engaged in all the programs," he recounts, adding that he felt encouraged to express, and take pride in, what made him different from his colleagues. With that came exposure to business leaders and the chance to influence them. "Just being myself more, while having the successful track record on the technical side, put me in a place where I had to rethink how I wanted to be part of corporate America. And I got more leadership opportunities out of that, not necessarily from my technical work but from public speaking. Going up to a podium and talking to large groups of people is something I had dreaded before. I felt like I had something to say, and to contribute."

The Pipeline Isn't the Problem

Judging by the persistent lack of employee engagement and increasing labor unrest, many people—not only those from groups that are overlooked for career advancement—feel their employers don't value their contributions. Certainly, people want higher pay, better working conditions, and more recognition for what they do. But that isn't the whole story. I have had hundreds of conversations in which people have told me about the emotional armor they put on every day before going to work and how it weighs on them.

The way business is conducted in their workplace, and how they are treated, tells them that, like Sullivan, they cannot be themselves. Maybe they struggle silently with their emotions because colleagues expect them to provide an opinion on every negative news story about someone in a group they identify with. Perhaps they are wrestling with a newly diagnosed disability but are afraid to disclose it because doing so would change how colleagues behave around them. Or they fear speaking up about threats to their physical and mental health or safety.

When people can't be who they really are, everyone bears the cost. People who are using their energy to maintain a mask can't be fully productive, creative, and innovative. Instead they are under constant stress, which affects their health, their performance, and consequently the performance rating they receive, which affects their wealth. It's no wonder so many people, having been through a pandemic, economic change, extreme weather, and social unrest, are rethinking what they want from work and going to look for it.

Meanwhile, we have an aging workforce that is leading to competition for labor and leadership globally. According to Korn Ferry, a lack of labor due to an aging population will cost the global economy $8.5 trillion by 2030, "equivalent to the combined GDP of Germany and Japan."[4] Deloitte reported that 80 percent of executives in focus groups view "leadership readiness" as "the biggest internal barrier to achieve their future strategies."[5] This isn't a pipeline problem; it's an inclusion problem. An analysis by consultancy Bain & Company found, for example, that in high-income countries, workers fifty-five and older will soon constitute almost one-fourth of the workforce.[6] But only a small percentage of firms today have recruitment, training, benefits, or retention programs that include these workers, who have different motivations, incentives, and needs than younger employees.

The challenge for organizations becomes even more pronounced when you think about who is missing from leadership and management. Consider that in the United States, half of all workers are women.[7] While there are gender imbalances in the workforce in key industries (such as manufacturing) that make fewer women available for leadership jobs, they are still not being appointed to leadership roles in proportion to their presence. This is true even in industries where there are plenty of women. A 2019 study found that although women hold nearly 80 percent of US health care services jobs, only 19 percent of hospitals are led by them.[8] Meanwhile, an analysis of employee data from twenty-four companies in the United States found that Blacks represented 14 percent of employees but held only 6 percent of executive roles.[9] Another study, which looked at the path to top management and board appointments in the Fortune 100, noted that senior executive roles (such as general counsel or human resources) held by women and racial minorities offered less potential for them to advance to CEO or become board directors.[10] If you aren't appointing more diverse leaders and managers, it isn't because they aren't there. It's because you aren't opening the door to them.

The consultancy McKinsey & Company found not only that women and racial and ethnic minorities are less likely to feel included in their organizations compared to all respondents, but also that inclusion is a problem generally. Only 44 percent of respondents with roles ranging from entry level through vice president feel very included in their companies, compared to 70 percent of senior leaders who do.[11] That's a huge disconnect between leaders and the people they lead. If middle managers, especially, do not feel welcome and included across the board, organizations will struggle to keep them—and this will diminish the bench of future leaders.

The experience of former Xerox CEO Ursula Burns is instructive. In her memoir *Where You Are Is Not Who You Are*, Burns, who was the first Black woman to become CEO of a Fortune 500 US company, writes about her journey from poverty to the C-suite. Burns observes that even after she became an executive, her White peers tended to look on her as an oddity. Her status and her performance were not enough to signal she belonged. Within Xerox, however, executives established a culture that welcomed and nurtured her. She thrived there because she was allowed—and encouraged—to be herself. She wore pants and styled her hair in a natural Afro. She asked pointed questions of leaders in team meetings, and they did not suppress her voice. Instead they understood her to be an independent thinker and problem solver with leadership potential. Senior leaders in the company, both Black and White men, chose her for roles that enabled her to learn how to lead, while showing her that people like her had a place at the top. The only time she contemplated leaving the company was when the CEO, whom she reported to as a member of the senior leadership team, showed no interest in her work or her point of view. That CEO left, and colleagues she trusted convinced her to stay.[12]

The Hallmarks of a Welcoming and Inclusive Culture

We behave differently when we are in a library versus a bar. We can modulate our behavior in different environments and still be authentic if the rules and norms of the place allow us to be. A welcoming and inclusive workplace is no different. These examples of organizational policies and messaging, and the day-to-day behavior of people, signal that individuals are free to be themselves:

- They are free to express their points of view without fear.
- Every person is treated with respect. Because respect means something different to each individual, many organizations define what it means for the organization, so the behavior expected is clear.

- People do not have to hide or downplay essential aspects of themselves, such as parenthood, race, ethnicity, religion, class, or sexual orientation, to fit in.
- Individuals are evaluated, recognized, and rewarded according to what they contribute, rather than external characteristics (not only gender or race but also factors like where they went to school, where they grew up, or their friendships or club memberships).
- Leaders and managers consider what each employee needs to perform at their highest potential and help them reach it. This is equity. For example, some employees may need opportunities to develop their public speaking abilities; others might need flexible schedules to care for a child or parent. You're providing resources and benefits based on the needs of individuals and different groups of people.
- Individuals are responsible for upholding these principles in their daily interactions, in their decisions about work assignments, when giving performance reviews, when setting pay, when offering promotions, and when communicating.

Notice the emphasis is on individuals and what they need to be at their best. Inclusion is not about any group of people. When organizations focus on inclusion, they improve the workplace for everyone. Notice also that responsibility is universal. Everyone, from the CEO to the lowest-level employee, is expected to behave inclusively—expected to be a role model— and no one is exempt.

If your approach to diversity, equity, and inclusion is limited to enforcing the law, adjudicating internal complaints, or burnishing the organization's image (or your own), you aren't making your organization a better place for anyone. Compliance-focused cultures are often not welcoming ones because they are based on proscribing a set of negative behaviors that aren't always well defined rather than encouraging people to treat each other as worthy of honor and respect. Meanwhile, people can be excluded in ways that will never be reported to HR and aren't against the law. As a simple example, think about the (usually male) leaders who think they are doing a favor for female subordinates who are parents when they decide not to give them tough assignments, ask them to travel, invite them to present to customers or board members, or ask them to join committees.

Natalie Alhonte Braga, director of strategy for Latin America with the global law firm Willkie Farr & Gallagher, recounts that when she worked for a strategic communications firm, she was handling "all the crisis accounts." When she got pregnant,

> all of a sudden, I started to get spared the stressful accounts, and it wasn't through a conversation with my boss about having a high-risk pregnancy and needing to take it easy. . . . And then there are the comments that people make.
>
> I travel a ton, and people say things like, oh, how does your son feel about you traveling? Or, I won't have you come in for that because you've been traveling so much. I don't want to take you away from your family.
>
> It seems kind on the surface, but really what you're saying is that you're unable to handle your personal life on your own, and I need to help you.[13]

People may need time at different points in their careers to take care of their families, manage an illness, or otherwise focus more on their personal lives than on work. But when a manager decides an employee cannot continue performing at a high level without talking to that employee about whether they are truly, if temporarily, constrained, they are unilaterally putting up a barrier to that employee's advancement. Even if such decisions are well intentioned, they take power away from the employee to decide about their own life. This is even truer if they also do not talk to that employee about how scaling back their involvement might affect their career goals. Not only is the manager depriving the employee of future opportunities for career growth and wealth, but they are also depriving their organization of the employee's future insights.

Here is another well-intentioned and common example with significant consequences that many individuals have shared with me: a decision to exclude the only woman or ethnic minority on a team from a social hour after a team meeting. They think they are protecting their teammate—assuming, without asking, that this person would not be comfortable with the activity or the venue. But by doing so, they remove the opportunity to bond with and learn from them. It can be uncomfortable to ask your colleague whether they want to go to a bar when they don't drink alcohol, if they will be the only non-White person, or where the entertainment is designed to appeal primarily to straight men. The answer may or may not lead you to find a different activity. However, if you are welcoming and model inclusion, you will not only endorse difference and show people how to embrace it; you will also make room for people to have uncomfortable conversations without shame, blame, or punishment.

In the context of practices that help an organization succeed, conversations about how people are treated because of their intrinsic characteristics aren't personal, even when they happen between individuals. They are about what needs to happen to make the workplace better for the people who do the work. When we ask people to be role models for diversity, equity, and inclusion, we may be asking them to act contrary to ingrained beliefs, or to change behavior that they are comfortable with and may think of as benign (like the manager taking away Alhonte Braga's "stressful" accounts). They may find this difficult. Just because we ask people to do things that an organization's leaders have decided is necessary for the good of the organization, that doesn't mean they will be happy about it. But with patience and attention, we can coach most people to behave differently.

Years ago I worked at a company where colleagues would shun or threaten LGBTQ+ employees if they revealed their identities. We needed to make them feel welcome; we couldn't afford to lose their talent or discourage anyone from coming to work for us. Our general counsel, whose religious beliefs opposed homosexuality, was struggling with this. My way to help him become more comfortable interacting with people he knew were homosexual was to ask him to be the executive sponsor of a lecture during Pride month by Kevin Jennings, a well-known author, educator, and advocate for LGBTQ+ youth. Jennings would share his personal story growing up and coming out as the gay son of a preacher. I had arranged similar talks by women, Black, and Asian speakers to share their experiences to help leaders, managers, and employees learn about people who differed from them.

To prepare the executive team, I gave a copy of Jennings's book, *Mama's Boy, Preacher's Son*, to each of them so they could become familiar with the ideas he would talk about and the language he would use. In addition, I briefed Jennings, as I did all of our speakers, about the business, its leadership, our employees, and our successes and challenges with diversity, equity, and inclusion. I shared why we had chosen him to speak, and what we hoped to achieve from his visit. We discussed what he would share from the book and his work, as well as actions our audience could take once they returned to their offices. I also arranged for Jennings and the general counsel to have dinner with me before the event, so they could get to know each other as people and connect with each other as fellow humans. Meanwhile, I created trust with the general counsel by assuring him I understood his discomfort and its source, and I would not judge him for it or his beliefs. I would be on call to answer his questions, provide relevant materials to increase his understanding and comfort, and keep him informed of any event-related developments.

The event was controversial: at the time, same-sex marriage was not legal in many states and countries where we operated, and many people in the company and the local community held beliefs that were like the general counsel's. Leading up to it, although many people in the company responded with support, I received enough threatening emails that I became concerned about my physical safety. I needed security to walk me out of the office every day. I kept Jennings informed of these developments so he had ample time to absorb the information and share how he felt. Because he had experienced similar situations before, he was also able to advise us on how to manage it.

And though it could have happened another way, the backlash flipped a switch for the general counsel. He stepped up as a leader rather than as an individual with a particular set of beliefs. He accepted that his duty to the company, as a lawyer and an executive, was to ensure every employee was treated equally and equitably (which were values he also held), and that this was essential to attracting and retaining the people we needed to be successful. He did a masterful job leading the event, which turned out to be our most profound. Many of the over two hundred global attendees—the most at any of our events to that point—were visibly moved. They asked a lot of questions and were generous with their glowing feedback afterward. The general counsel was at ease: poised, engaging, funny, human. And committed. When one employee behaved threateningly, the general counsel stood by our corporate values and released the man from his duties. Later, the company was invited to serve on the board of GLSEN, the organization Jennings cofounded to help schools create and maintain harassment-free learning environments for LGBTQ+ students.

Like the general counsel, those who are motivated to help their organizations succeed—and who want to succeed themselves—will step up as role models when it is clear what they need to do, they have guidance on how to do it, and their efforts are supported. As with any other shift in how business is done, those that cannot adapt will leave or be let go— not because they have unpopular ideas or because they feel uncomfortable around people who differ from them, but because they are unable or unwilling to demonstrate the values that the company reveres. The rest will thrive together.

Start with Values

I once heard the late Madeleine Albright, the first female US secretary of state, observe that like wallpaper, values are merely beautiful to look at unless people are living up to them.[14] Albright was addressing a meeting of corporate directors and urging us to uphold American values internationally. But the sentiment applies broadly. For values to be more than wallpaper—for them to have meaning and inspire action—leaders and managers have to embody them consistently both in how they behave as individuals and in their business practices.

Many organizations say they value people, or put them first, or some variation on this theme. They may even say they value diversity. Values such as integrity, trust, innovation, and accountability also put people and how they treat one another at the center of business decisions. If senior executives take these seriously as core values, they have a gateway for examining how they hire, develop, and select leaders. You will not be able to practice any values consistently unless you prioritize the behavior that you seek when you choose your teams.

As Patrick Lencioni, a management consultant specializing in organizational health, has written, if any core values, no matter what they are, are "going to really take hold in your organization, [they] need to be integrated into every employee-related process—hiring methods, performance management systems, criteria for promotions and rewards, and even dismissal policies. From the first interview to the last day of work, employees should be constantly reminded that core values form the basis for every decision the company makes."[15]

Dyann Heward-Mills is CEO of Heward-Mills, a small business that provides data protection services to companies globally. She also advises the European Union on such matters. When she founded her firm, she connected her commitment to human rights with a mission to keep companies' data secure and safeguard individuals' privacy.

She was drawn to the data protection field while studying computer and communications law. "It was partly about commerce and how organizations can use information and drive innovation, but it was also about . . .

the importance of treating information relating to individuals with dignity and protecting that special thing, that privacy, that area of our lives that we hold very dear to ourselves," she explains.[16] The values of the firm reflect her pursuit of fairness and equality in society. How the company makes hiring decisions, how it determines compensation, and how her diverse team works together "all ties in around respecting humanity, acting ethically, acting with respect for each other, supporting each other," she says. "We want them to earn well, to have a good quality of life, to provide for their families, provide for their communities . . . it's about changing the lives of those that interact with us and the lives of our clients, too."

It's easy to see Heward-Mills as a role model.

Five Essential Characteristics of Welcoming and Inclusive Cultures

As a leader or manager of people, you are also a role model. What kind of role model you are depends on what you do—or don't do. Your behavior sets the standard for your team, your department, your division, or the whole organization. And it helps to create the culture.

You aren't telling people what to think. You are showing them how they can be and, critically for the workplace, what it takes to be successful. When leaders make clear what they expect, by writing it into policy and talking about it, and they show how to achieve it—including what they do when they fall short of their own expectations—their people will rise to the challenge. Your business culture, after all, is the sum of the behavior of the people who work there.

It's important to have a vision for what you want your welcoming culture to look like because a leader without a vision is like a cricket player without a bat. Researchers have identified a range of inclusive leadership attributes that shape the work environment.[17] Practitioners like me have used this research to define lists of traits or behaviors for inclusive leaders to model. In my work, I focus on five. You can think about these as a mini framework for modeling a welcoming and inclusive culture within our ABCD framework. You'll see below how practicing these behaviors looks from the point of view of a team or organization.

These are the five essential characteristics:

Being curious: encouraging people to ask questions of themselves and others about processes and decisions that affect the team, its work, and the business.

Being aware: exploring what your team, and your organizations, are missing about people who differ from yourselves, or from the majority, so you can see your blind spots.

Being courageous: making it safe to discuss a broad array of subjects (including seemingly unpopular ones), to make unconventional choices, and to experiment.

Being committed: agreeing the organization will inspect and update its systems, processes, policies, and practices to make them more inclusive.

Being collaborative: working effectively with your team, your peers, and your partners to discover what inspires and motivates them and helps them achieve their goals.

I coach my clients that these behaviors are interrelated. Start practicing one, and it will lead you to the others.

Being Curious

In any endeavor, we won't get far unless we inform ourselves about our goals and how to reach them. If you have tackled any hard challenge, you know the path is rarely straightforward or predictable. Good leaders, managers, and employees will be curious about everything that affects their business and their work and how they can be more successful.

A few years ago I worked with Nancy McGaw, senior advisor of the Aspen Institute Business & Society Program, to prepare her for a virtual event. I learned from her that asking questions is a trait that great leaders and thinkers have in common, and it's a crucial step toward ushering in change. In fact, she observed, some leaders have so many questions that they fill their meeting agendas with them.[18] When we are curious and ask more questions, we are more likely to see more, understand more, do more, and miss less. We get insight into our assumptions about people and their potential.

When I worked with Michael Frank at Monsanto, I gave a presentation to his team that included the basic concepts of diversity, equity, and inclusion and the case for them in the company. He asked me to say more about what inclusion means. As an example, I explained that introverts and extroverts have different communication styles, and in meetings extroverts tend to dominate because they are comfortable speaking spontaneously. Introverts, on the other hand, may not speak up often because they are uncomfortable speaking spontaneously. And the leaders running the meetings don't notice.

When I finished, one of the two women on his leadership team raised her hand. She shared that she was an introvert, and this was why she didn't always contribute. For Frank it was an epiphany. For the first time, he understood he had someone on his team he was not hearing from often enough and that he had never asked her why, nor had he made a point of asking for her input. He realized that he didn't always hear from her whenever the team discussed an issue and made decisions. This is how he came to understand the bigger concept.

There were a couple of immediate results. We partnered on a workshop for his team to learn about identifying biases and assumptions within themselves, the team, and the organization. He also set expectations with his global leadership team and HR that developing women and advancing them into leadership roles when there were opportunities for which they were qualified were priorities.

Frank and his team could move forward because he asked a question in front of his team. Although Frank is one of the most inclusive people leaders—and one of the most committed to diversity, equity, and inclusion—that I have been privileged to work with, he is still not perfect, and he wasn't embarrassed to show them he did not know it all. In doing so, he gave everyone on his team permission to do the same. And he showed humility, which goes hand in hand with curiosity. We are unlikely to be curious in the first place if we think we have nothing to learn. If knowledge is what you know, and wisdom is acknowledging what you don't, being curious leads to learning—which is the bridge between the two.

Curiosity starts with *why*. When we are children learning about the world, we ask this question about everything. It's one of the best ways to uncover information, yet many of us seem to have forgotten how. I like to borrow from a methodology pioneered at the automobile manufacturer Toyota, which they called the Five Whys. These are five *why* questions that anyone can ask to get to the root of a problem without pointing fingers or placing blame.[19] We can start by asking, Why is it important for us to include a greater variety of people in leadership? Then, Why is our leadership team not representative of the talent available in our company, community, nation, or region? And further, Why do I not see the people in my organization who differ from most of my workforce: perhaps those who have lived outside my country, went to a community college, speak multiple languages, grew up in a multigenerational household? The answers will lead you to other questions, which may or may not begin with *why*. Such as, What are truly the steps to becoming a leader in my organization?

When you ask questions as a leader, you give permission to everyone else in your organization to ask questions as well. Thus, you shift the culture from one that might never have talked openly about diversity to one where people think about it and talk about it in the course of regular business.

Being Aware

While we can be experts in many areas, we cannot know everything. It is one reason we spend a lot of time, energy, and resources hiring people. We need their insights, the collective wisdom of the team, to run our organizations. Admitting what we don't know is the first step to becoming aware of our blind spots. As I've said, each of us has our unique view of the world and how to move in it, and it isn't limited to what we assume about other people. We are always missing information about others' experiences, but we don't routinely think about where our ideas about people or anything else come from.

Anyone can help their colleagues discover their blind spots, as this story from Aileen Casanave illustrates. Casanave is a technology attorney, business executive, teacher, and board member of several nonprofit organizations in Silicon Valley. At the beginning of her career, she was one of two women on a legal team at a defense contractor. Her female colleague traveled often, leaving Casanave as the only woman at their weekly staff meetings. She saw these meetings as opportunities to learn by listening attentively, observing closely, and modeling her colleagues' behavior. However, she observed one pattern that she could not model: their practice of continuing business conversations during bathroom breaks. By the time she returned to the conference room after these breaks, her teammates had made decisions, and she had not been included.

Casanave decided to call them out in a humorous way. One day, she followed her male colleagues to the restroom, talking as they walked to signal that she intended to follow them in. "If you are going to continue the staff meeting in the restroom, I'm going to join you," she recounts.[20] Assuming she was kidding, they quipped they were just talking about baseball. But by taking a stand, and behaving as a role model, "it proved a point— that it wasn't conscious to them they were excluding me," she says. She didn't have to go into the men's room; they got the message and stopped discussing business when she wasn't present. And the moment turned into a standing joke: whenever it was time for a restroom break, they would ask if she was coming with them.

You may not have an Aileen Casanave on your team, willing to take the risk of pointing out what you have not seen. And in any case, as a role model, you will want to show your team how they can do this for themselves. Here is a thought experiment to help. I call it the balcony-ballroom effect.

Think of a ballroom with a balcony. There are people dancing on the floor, and people observing from the balcony above. If you are on the balcony, you can see people moving about: a smiling couple twirling across the floor, another struggling to find rhythm, and someone on the sidelines tapping their feet. From your comfortable seat, you might judge them. Perhaps, because you judge yourself a good dancer, you decide the first couple has danced together many times and the rhythm-chasing partners do not know each other well. You assume the person on their own has no partner and you think how embarrassing it must be for them.

You could be wrong about all of them. Maybe the first couple learned to dance separately—they have experience, but this is their first date. One of the second couple may be recovering from an injury and is dancing for the first time in many months. The lone person may be waiting for their spouse, who has gone to change into dancing shoes. By the same token, the dancers might look at you above them and, if you are middle-aged or elderly, they might judge you to be infirm. But perhaps you're up there because you're hot and simply wanted to get out of the crowd for a while.

We are all either on the dance floor or on the balcony at one time or another, and we never have the whole story about what we see. But we can make a habit of catching ourselves when we are thinking and deciding about a person based on our preconceived ideas—that is, our biases. One way to shed light on where your biases lie is to think of the five people you rely on the most and whether the race, gender, education, sexual orientation, and other characteristics of those people differ from yours. I do this exercise with participants in my workshops about inclusive leadership and workplaces. They often find that they rely on others who are most like them—which, as I've said, is not a surprise, given that we are predisposed to this.

There is nothing wrong with relying on people who are like us, but the exercise reveals how insulated we can be without realizing it. Even if we are not intentionally biased against anyone, we get the same results if we neglect to consider the viewpoints of people who have had different experiences than us, or if we discount those viewpoints because they don't agree with ours. Once we become aware of our biases—our blind spots—we start to see differently. We begin to notice when a perspective is missing, and we seek it out. We begin to notice, also, when we say or do something that has excluded our colleagues. As we do, we'll engage our curiosity again, asking ourselves why people from certain demographic groups are missing and what role our blind spots have played in discouraging them from contributing.

In a culture where people become comfortable acknowledging their own biases and collegially pointing out others', it's a logical step to identify blind spots in the organization—the systems, policies, and processes that are preventing a wider range of people from becoming leaders. Both take courage.

Being Courageous

It takes courage to admit to ourselves, not to mention others, when we lack knowledge, or when we are wrong. In a business setting, we tend to be rewarded for what we know and to lose status when we make mistakes, especially due to ignorance. Leaders may feel pressure to hide what they don't know or present a facade of certainty. People may also fear being punished if they critique colleagues' behavior or organizational practices.

Even though we have decades of research about the benefits to organizations when people feel safe revealing their ignorance or expressing dissent, the business culture—influenced by leader behavior—does not always support it.[21] Therefore, as individuals, we may not always feel secure enough to reveal our lack of knowledge or understanding or to risk conflict. Because conversations about diversity, equity, and inclusion can be fraught with emotion and politically polarizing, many people are afraid to talk about their experiences, observations, or concerns. It's up to leaders to model how these discussions can take place without fear or judgment. It doesn't matter who you are; none of us is comfortable sharing when doing so could make our peers think poorly of us. Rejection hurts when it threatens our identity.

Michael Frank showed courage, along with curiosity and humility, when he asked me to explain what I meant by *inclusion*, and when he acknowledged that his bias about who participates in meetings had resulted in a woman being left out. So did the technology executive in one of my workshops who shared that the five people he relied on the most are all Boomers like him; he was lacking the input from two younger generations (Gen X and Millennials) when he made decisions.

It may take courage, as well, to stand up for individuals who differ from you, or to challenge a practice that excludes groups of people from participating fully, when it may create dissension on your team. A CEO I know recounted an instance of a team member making a homophobic remark to him in the presence of another executive whom the CEO knew to be gay. The gay executive had not been open about his identity and, in such a case, many people might let an offensive remark slide rather than escalate into a conflict. Instead, the CEO shot back, "If you ever make that remark here again, you're fired."

You may not have the same power to dictate behavior as this CEO. But when you have the courage to set expectations for how your team members behave and to point out when someone violates those expectations, you become a role model for everyone. A nonjudgmental approach is to ask, "Are you aware that what you have just said is contrary to the welcoming and inclusive culture we are trying to create for everyone?" This creates an opening to learn about that person's worldview and why they showed up as they did. You can then navigate the conversation to a meaningful outcome.

Being Committed

When you start on the path to creating a welcoming and inclusive culture, you commit to examining everything about how your organization operates. You will do this as part of a team with every other leader and manager; it's rarely possible for any manager to change a system, policy, or practice single-handedly.

I worked with a company to help them find the places in their strategic plan where they were leaving people out. We focused in part on their growth strategy, which emphasized merging with or acquiring other companies. The head of their mergers and acquisitions (M&A) division told me they found suitable targets by asking bankers with whom they had existing relationships. Because I asked, they revealed that their bankers were White and were connecting them only with companies that were also run by White people. As a result, they were unaware of the opportunities to buy companies run by people who are not White, and which might be even more attractive for them to acquire. (In 2020, 19.9 percent of small businesses in the United States were minority-owned.)[22] This insight resulted in the M&A division leader, who was White and heterosexual, committing to seeking businesses founded by non-White people, LGBTQ+ people, people with diverse religious beliefs, and people who have physical disabilities.

As you can see, the leaders at this company looked beyond the obvious areas, such as how you hire, develop, and promote your people. You and your colleagues will also look at how you create and execute your strategy; which products and services you pursue; how you manufacture, sell, and deliver those products and services; how you choose suppliers and partners; and the teams you assemble to meet with prospective customers or partners. You may be able to make some changes relatively quickly, while others will take time. But the only way that your workforce and stakeholders will know that you are serious is to see that you follow through with changes that can be sustained even when business conditions shift, and that you commit to a continuous process of examination.

Aileen Casanave and her colleagues were comfortable with their bathroom joke—it created camaraderie. But if another woman, or an LBGTQ+ person, or someone from a more formal culture had joined the team, it might not have had the same effect. A new person might have considered the banter rude. Or they might have thought Casanave was being sexually harassed, even if she explained the backstory. Either way, they might have felt they didn't belong—and it would have been time to put the teasing to rest.

Commitment starts at the top. When employees and managers see leaders bake diversity, equity, and inclusion into their decision-making, and they have the information and tools to do the same, they will follow suit and trust that what they are doing is necessary to achieve their business goals, even if they do not share the conviction that creating a more inclusive organization is the right thing to do. Together, you commit to nothing less than the inspection and adjustment of the relevant systems, policies, and practices so that people—employees, customers, investors, community members, and other stakeholders—become central to them.

Being Collaborative

Inclusion eludes many leaders and managers because they don't collaborate with the people on their teams to help them perform at their best or advance their careers. And they spend little time finding out what they need. According to a Gallup study, only 30 percent of American employees strongly agree that their managers involve them in setting their goals. Nearly half reported they get feedback only a few times a year or less.[23] It's hardly surprising that people leaders have blind spots that interfere with their ability to know what anyone on their team thinks, feels, or wants.

However, many organizations have moved from annual performance reviews to regular—ideally weekly—check-ins between leaders and their direct reports. If this is the practice at your organization, you can expand these conversations beyond sharing updates about work progress and get to know your direct reports as human beings. This is the starting point for making people feel welcome and valued.

You are learning who they are—what inspires and motivates them, what they value, how they think, what they struggle with, what they hope to achieve, and how they feel. Because we are multidimensional people, we bring our values, culture, religion, style, health, love for our families and desire to care for them, sports loyalties, community involvement, favorite foods, music, movies—the list goes on—to work with us, too. Every aspect of how we experience the world informs how we interact with other people and how we solve problems, as well as where and how we work most effectively.

Leaders who see our differences can align our strengths and skills with the needs of the organization and invest in what each person needs to become better at what they do. "Managing towards your business goals is great and you can be effective to a certain point, but if you want to really raise leaders and effective teams, and influence people in a lasting manner . . . you've got to get behind exactly what's making them tick, and then weave that into how you're successful," observes Michael Santa Maria, a partner with Baker McKenzie who leads teams that provide legal services to companies that operate internationally.[24]

His goal for every relationship is to have mutual care, trust, and respect. "You would never let them down. That's the commitment that people need to feel and then it needs to be genuine," he says. The same goes for clients. He tunes in, as well, to the stresses team members may be facing. These may relate to belonging to a group that has faced discrimination, being a parent, or some other challenge—and the solutions are unique to each person. Santa Maria positions himself as an advisor they can trust to help them navigate their career path, taking their circumstances into account.

"Ultimately, the team that you have is the team that you've invested time into putting together," he says. "It certainly makes me look good that I'm able to bring along high potential people . . . and have them really knock it out of the park."

Good leaders and managers may decide for themselves to be collaborators with the people on their teams. But when organizations instill this behavior as a corporate management practice, it becomes part of the culture. Managers can learn how to identify employees' needs and to clear obstacles from their path. They can also be evaluated on how effective they are and advised how to improve if needed.

A story from Hubert Joly, the former chairman and CEO of Best Buy, in his book about his leadership philosophy, illustrates how leaders and managers can collaborate with their team members and become role models for the organization. He writes that when a regional manager at Best Buy focused on setting personalized goals for each sales associate, determining what they needed to learn individually to improve their skills and explore their future career paths, revenue increased 10 percent over the course of one year. "We rolled out his approach nationwide, and it caught like wildfire," Joly continues. "Every month, there was a call with top performers across the country so they could share their best practices. The new approach lifted skills and amplified motivation. It was one of the most critical changes we adopted during the turnaround."[25]

Focus on People When Making Decisions

We began this chapter by observing that the systems, policies, and practices of an organization determine the workplace culture and who is welcome in it. Then we delved into defining culture, what it means to be welcoming, and the behavior that leaders and managers should model for their teams to create an inclusive environment.

There is one more piece: a process that embeds diversity, equity, and inclusion into business decisions by putting people first. Some organizations use a human-centered design process when developing new products, services, and information technology to "keep users' wants, pain points, and preferences front of mind during every phase of the process."[26] Similar principles can apply to other decision-making processes in any area of the organization.

Discover

- Who is affected?
- Do I understand how they feel and what they want?
- Have I asked them?

Define

- What frustrates the affected people?
- What problem do they need me to solve?
- Do different stakeholders view the problem differently?

Develop

- Have I included the affected people when brainstorming and testing solutions?
- Have I made it safe for anyone to question current practices, the ideas for changing them, and the process?
- Have I allowed multiple solutions to be considered?

Deliver

- Who is communicating the solutions?
- Do different stakeholders need different information?
- How will I get feedback on the solution and the process?

Figure 4.1
Leaders and managers can embed diversity, equity, and inclusion into their decisions through a process that incorporates empathy with what employees and other stakeholders need.

We embed diversity, equity, and inclusion into decisions when we deliberately account for the differences among groups of people. For example, when a manufacturer upgrades its equipment, it can study how people with a wide range of body types operate the current machines and choose new ones that a greater variety of people can safely operate. To apply this to your organization:

- Start with discovery. Examine what you know about the people who will be affected by the decision, your assumptions about them, and the extent to which you have already sought their input. Then approach them with empathy. Your goal is to find their challenges, which may not be the same for every group.

- Next, define the problem you are solving by listening, observing, and asking questions of people in different groups. Go into the field to see and hear about the outcomes of existing practices firsthand. Learn how the challenges that people face differ according to their demographic characteristics. Figure out what frustrates them, and the sources they identify for these issues.

- When you have done your research and defined the problem, you will be ready to develop your solution. As you do, continue to seek input from the wide range of people who have a stake in the outcome. If they are not in the room, invite them, and make it safe for them to question both the ideas and the process. Consider the barriers you may have to address to change current practices.

- Finally, deliver your solution or your decision—and communicate it to all your stakeholders. Consider who is receiving the message, who will deliver it (someone stakeholders feel represents them, whom they trust) and whether different groups need different information. Create a way for stakeholders to give feedback as their needs evolve.

Notice that throughout the process, the person leading it serves as a role model for how to empathize: to put people and their needs at the center of any decision. In the discovery phase, they encourage team members to be curious about what affects their work and notice their assumptions. They keep asking questions to define the problem they need to solve. As they develop solutions, they make it safe for people to express unpopular ideas and experiment. At every stage, they collaborate with their teammates and peers to find solutions that address their needs. And when they deliver a

If you aren't appointing more diverse leaders and managers, it isn't because they aren't there. It's because you aren't opening the door to them.

solution or decision, they show their commitment to making the organization more inclusive.

Questions for Creating a Culture of Role Models

When you live with something for a long time, you don't know it has lost its luster. Fresh eyes see things as they are now. Today's workforce is diverse, and in the future it will be even more so.

Without an inclusive culture that welcomes people representing humanity in all its differences, organizations will struggle to attract the talent they need to thrive. Some questions you can ask to begin building an inclusive culture of role models for your organization include:

- How are we practicing our values internally and with our stakeholders? Are they embedded in the employee life cycle, in how we develop and select leaders, and how we choose external partners?
- Do we encourage employees to ask questions to improve their understanding of each other's needs and differences and to become aware of their blind spots?
- What are we doing to become aware of our blind spots as a team and as an organization?
- How do we support people when they exercise courage to reveal what they don't know or question our practices, including when they say something that is taboo?
- Who among my direct reports is not a role model for the organization's values? What do they need to become one?
- Which inclusive behaviors do I need to work on to be a better role model?
- Are the role models in my organization representative of the workforce?
- Whose voices are not being heard?

5 Pillar D: How to Define Objectives and Outcomes with Data

A Fortune 500 CEO once said to me, "When it comes to diversity and inclusion, we get the business case, we get that we must demand diverse slates of job candidates, we get the need for training to reduce unconscious biases." After pausing and sighing, he continued, "But for God's sake, after all the time and resources we have devoted to it, we have very little to show for it." His frustration is woefully common. And one big reason is that the language of diversity, equity, and inclusion, with its emphasis on moral principles and human feeling, has little in common with the language of business decisions—data and metrics. Leaders and managers don't know what to do or say because without data to describe the problem they need to solve and metrics to show them whether they are making progress, they cannot integrate inclusion into their jobs, which are to run the organization, make a profit, or serve a mission.

Principles of justice, fairness, and equality can and should be a guiding force for business decisions; in fact, many leaders and managers wrestle daily with the effect their decisions have on people and the planet. As humans, they want to do the right thing by their stakeholders, including their employees. This may even be inspiration for the core values we referenced in the previous chapter. But even when they commit as humans to improving the world, their organizations cannot continue unless they achieve their business objectives.[1] This is why every business function uses data to describe the opportunities it is pursuing, the progress it is making, and its contribution to organizational goals. And data must contribute to sustaining investment because there is competition for limited resources. In every business, leaders and managers have choices about where to invest time, money, and attention; they aren't likely to continue dedicating these to any area that doesn't help to achieve their goals. Nor are they likely to change their behavior unless they can see that doing so makes the business more successful.

Diversity, equity, and inclusion does not differ from any other business function. For it to be embraced as one, it needs to operate like one. It needs to show what it contributes with a variety of data and rigorous analysis. Pillar D supports the rest of the framework like a load-bearing wall carries the weight of a structure. You need data to execute the first three pillars.

Every businessperson uses data daily to communicate about what they are doing and whether they are achieving their goals. We know how to respond to what numbers tell us. A CEO reviews data on customers, competitors, technological advances, and market trends in order to shape strategic objectives, cultivate the executive management culture, and maximize long-term market position. A COO reviews key performance indicators (KPIs) to evaluate the effectiveness of operational controls and adjusts resources, processes, technologies, or vendors to improve efficiency, reduce risk, or improve market position. A sales manager who learns revenues are down for the week directs her team to work on closing more deals.

Data drives powerful and meaningful decisions. Milton Davenport, a Chicago-based endodontist with a three-office practice, changed how he compensated his staff when he learned that some hourly employees were less productive. They were trying to stretch out their hours—and thus their income. "It makes sense. You want to make sure you get enough hours to support your family," he told me. Davenport put them on salary at a level that enables them to pay their bills. "You can work thirty hours, or forty or fifty hours; this is what you're going to get paid."[2] In doing so, he made his workplace more equitable for employees who were struggling financially and improved how his people and business performed.

You may or may not be able to change employee compensation. But your business data offers a powerful means to show how your organization can benefit from having more diverse leaders and managers, and the talented individuals in every demographic category who you are leaving out. When you know, you can change your operations in ways you would never think to do if all you had to go on were the broad slices of workforce demographic data in your organization's diversity report.

> Diversity, equity, and inclusion does not differ from any other business function.

Typically, all aggregate data reveals is the extent to which the overall diversity of the workforce is progressing toward the organization's goals for hiring people in whatever categories they have focused on. Organizations may segment this data by role so people leaders can see how diverse different levels of management are. But in my experience, they often don't. They may not even look at data that is unrelated to categories that receive public or legal scrutiny, such as gender, race, or ethnicity. Therefore, they won't see the full range of diversity in their workforce, including people with LGBTQ+ identities, physical disabilities, or native languages other than English, or who are from different generations. Nor will the data tell them where any of these employees are in the organization, their expertise, or their potential for leadership.

It's even more unusual to analyze employee demographic data with business and financial data. For example, managers don't routinely ask their HR partners for help studying the business results of teams led by women compared to men; nor does HR usually think about delving into personnel data this way. They might track broad categories, such as the number of White or non-White people employed in a business unit, or in management generally, or by location. But this is a surface-level analysis.

It's easy to calculate average pay gaps between women and men or Blacks and Whites in an organization, but numbers like these tell us nothing other than that we need to do more research. When we segment the data further, we may find that, in fact, salaries of women and men or Blacks and Whites in the same jobs are somewhat equal and, as we learned about Citi, the true problem is that women and Blacks aren't well represented at the top. Once you know that, you can determine how to solve it.

You can add more data about your operations, your customers, your suppliers, and your market and learn even more. You may find out, like Cartier, that women are spending more on your products and conclude that involving more women in sales and product development decisions would create more sales opportunities. Or you may observe, as one Fortune 500 bank I have worked with did, that you are missing opportunities to serve non-White customers. Data is rich with stories that illuminate the business problems and opportunities that a greater diversity of leaders can address. And I don't mean only numerical data.

Quantitative data can tell you what is happening and what people think about it, but it's difficult to learn why people do or think anything, or how they feel, from numbers alone. Moreover, surveys will never capture the answers to questions you never thought to ask. So you also need qualitative data—the stories you collect when you talk and listen to people. What they tell you about their day-to-day experience in the workplace and what makes them feel valued (or not) will bring the numbers to life and give them meaning. Numbers plus narrative equals insight.

One advantage to talking and listening is that you need nothing other than yourself and a notepad or recording device. (I recommend recordings and the transcripts you can create from them to capture the maximum amount of information accurately.) If your organization lacks much quantitative data about people that you can segment, or you do not have access to the tools or expertise you need to analyze it, this is a good place to start.

To connect diversity, equity, and inclusion; leadership and management; and business priorities, you need a rich collection of data besides your employee data—information about customers, finances, operations, and the market that HR departments are unlikely to collect themselves but that are available from sales and marketing, operations, finance, and other places in the organization. When you segment that data in all the ways that are relevant to your industry and your organization, you can understand the full range of perspectives you need on your team. Even if you don't have exactly the data you want, you are likely to have enough to see gaps, opportunities, and metrics that matter.

Your ultimate goal is to make data about diversity, equity, and inclusion relevant to every decision about business strategy and operations that involves people—which, to be frank, is every decision. As I said earlier, it's people who do the work. It's also people who will leave for better opportunities if you do not value them and what they contribute. Unless you see them, you won't know what—or who—you are missing.

The Data You Need Is Everywhere

In my corporate roles, I always started my work by understanding the business plan. Then I looked for opportunities to connect diversity, equity, and inclusion with that plan by analyzing the people data.

I segmented employees not only by demographic categories related to diversity but also by where they were in the company hierarchy, from the board level to the factory floor, their tenure in their role, their geographical location, and the parts of the organization where they worked. Then I could show leaders where different groups were underrepresented, at what levels and in which locations their careers were stalling, and the areas with the greatest opportunity to improve the organization by including a more diverse range of people in leadership and management. With additional data about sales, revenue, customer behavior, or productivity that I obtained from colleagues, I was able to tell stories about the company and its potential that weren't visible when looking at the aggregated data only. These stories offered a way forward: concrete reasons to change, a direction to go, and a way to measure how they were progressing.

For example, at the law firm Baker McKenzie, the (mostly male) leaders at the top and middle of the firm understood in principle that they needed to include more women in the partnership ranks and leadership. They were even under pressure from clients to do so. However, they tended to assume that women were less productive than men because of their childcare responsibilities, even if they were not always aware they held these beliefs.

Revenue per hour is an important measure of attorney performance, and the firm reported on this productivity data quarterly. I saw an opportunity to test whether or not the leaders' assumptions about women were true by segmenting this data according to gender, and our CFO, who owned this data, agreed. We broke out the revenue per hour that women and men generated, and we showed, contrary to what many male attorneys believed, that women contributed equally to men.

When we delved deeper and showed them the numbers by office and region, leaders across the firm could see that they were underutilizing their female employees. And we strengthened the case for making the firm more inclusive by changing how it operated and selected its partners and leaders. As is true of many law firms, women and men were about equally represented among associates, but not among partners, practice leaders, or firm leadership, so it was easy to see where we needed to focus.

As you can see from this example, using employee and financial data to illustrate how including more women could improve business performance accomplished what good intentions had not. Years earlier, the firm had set goals to appoint more women as partners and leaders, but it was not satisfied with its progress.

The analysis I provided was relatively simple, using existing data (employee demographics, employee performance, revenue) and a metric (productivity) that almost every organization tracks. It revealed a blind spot and pointed leaders toward the actions they could take to improve results. It connected inclusion of women with one of the firm's business priorities (maximizing productivity), and it became an entry point for engaging partners who ran local offices in the changes the firm would make to its culture and operations. We created a dashboard and scorecard that enabled these leaders to see where women were present or absent in partnership, management roles, and leadership in their locations. We rolled up the local data and presented it as part of the annual global partnership meeting, so it was always visible across the organization and usable by any people leader.

The person who leads diversity, equity, and inclusion in your organization should be familiar with how to use data. Their team will identify areas for research and present the findings, while data collection and analysis will be a collaborative effort with the stakeholders who own the needed information. Whether you are a C-level leader, a division or department head, or the manager of a team, partnering with the diversity, equity, and inclusion leader to develop deep, data-supported connections between people, business priorities, and performance will help you make more informed decisions. It bears repeating that your job as a leader is to ensure that the best people are in place to carry out your business priorities—and they come from everywhere. "At the end of the day, we need to perform," says Matt Downs, the co-CEO of Sandbox Industries, a venture capital firm that invests in agriculture, health care, and financial services startups. "If you say, 'I need an African American in the room,' or 'I need a woman in the room,' you're missing it. I need a brilliant thinker with a different background than mine, who brings a different perspective, who will help us make effective decisions. And if you're established on that philosophy, then you're going to move in the right direction."[3]

Five Categories of Data

Ideally, you will collect five categories of business data: internal data about employees, customers, finances, and operations, and external data about your industry or consumer trends. Then you will segment it and analyze it by the relevant demographic characteristics.

Below are examples of different sources of data from each category that you can use in your analysis. Depending on your role, you may already be

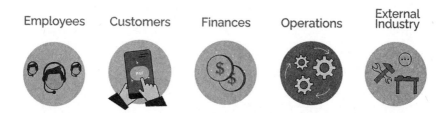

Employees   Customers   Finances   Operations   External Industry

Figure 5.1
Organizations collect five types of business data that can be used to understand who is missing from leadership and management.

familiar with some of this data, but you may not know how you can use it to further diversity, equity, and inclusion. These are not exhaustive lists. Nor should you be concerned if your organization collects only a few of the sources suggested. You can use whatever data you have and make plans to collect what you would like to have in the future. In addition, your organization may have data that is unique to it, its industry, or the markets where it operates. The most important criterion is that the data is meaningful to the business and that it is used to make decisions.

Employee Data
Employee data includes any information about employees that is tracked in human resources systems. These are some useful types of employee data:

Employee demographics: Many organizations keep data about employees' gender, age, and race or ethnicity. Yours may also have data about the tenure and level of employees. If you operate in more than one country, you may have data about the nationalities of your employees (with the caveat that data is subject to local privacy laws).

Performance evaluations: ratings of employees, leaders, and managers.

Employee satisfaction and engagement: this data comes from employee surveys.

Career progression: this includes movement up, down, across, and out of the organization, or lack of movement.

Benefits utilization: Data about the education, health and wellness, vacation, childcare, eldercare, lifestyle improvement perks, and other benefits employees use can provide insight into how different segments of the workforce access these resources and point to inequities that may affect their ability to advance. (At Monsanto, for example, we learned male scientists were more likely to take advantage of education benefits than women, which partly explained why men advanced faster.)

Leadership development assessments: these can come from both internal and external sources, such as executive search firms that conduct assessments for your leadership team.

Salary and wage distribution.

Employee net promotor score: this measures whether the employees and leaders would recommend your organization's products and services to others.

Spencer Rascoff, the cofounder of online residential real estate firm Zillow Group, has related that when the company dug into its hiring data, it learned that all-male interview teams were less likely to hire women, and the bias toward male candidates was particularly strong when hiring for technology roles. When they added one woman to the interview teams for technical positions, the teams chose more women. Where before they hired women only 14 percent of the time, including a female interviewer resulted in women being selected 40 percent of the time.[4]

If your organization does not collect employee demographic data, or you need more of it, you will want to begin collecting whatever you can legally where you operate. And don't forget qualitative data. From your listening sessions with employees you can develop a detailed picture of what motivates them, what demoralizes them, what helps them succeed or creates struggle. These conversations will point to actions to take and areas for further research.

Customer Data

Customer data includes any information about customers' behavior, preferences, and opinions about your organization. Sales, marketing, customer service, and product development teams are most likely to have this type of data:

- the products and services customers buy
- what matters to them when deciding what to purchase
- where, when, and how they shop, the time they spend on your website, and whether they engage with salespeople or customer service representatives before they buy

- how they pay for your products and services
- their participation in loyalty programs
- how they interact with your organization when they have questions or complaints, such as in person, by email, with a phone call, or via online chat
- customer experience metrics, which include net promoter scores (measuring how likely customers are to recommend the organization to others), customer satisfaction surveys, comments on social media, product reviews, and other feedback

Your organization may not collect demographic information about all of its customers, and not everyone feels comfortable disclosing this information. But to the extent that this data is available, you can segment it to learn how customers from different demographics behave and what they like or dislike about your products, services, and organization overall. In fact, many sales and marketing departments already segment customer data to inform their strategies and programs. If you are a senior leader or a middle manager, you are probably familiar with at least some of it already. In addition, sales, marketing, and product development teams may conduct focus groups, user experience testing, or other qualitative studies for insight into what customers value, what they struggle with, and what they would like to see your organization do differently. These insights are similar to what you would learn from talking with employees.

In 2015 the startup Doppler Labs was developing wireless earbuds with an app that would help users control sound quality, including a prototype for the Coachella music festival.[5] Executives noticed inquiries from potential customers about whether the devices could filter background noise so they could hear conversations better. They turned to K. R. Liu, a sales and marketing executive who had gained attention for her work with Pebble, a smartwatch pioneer, to enable people with hearing aids to control them through the watch. Liu had experienced severe hearing loss as an infant, and she was advocating for new hearing technologies that were more affordable and less noticeable. "I tried them, and I was like, oh my god, this is the new hearing aid," she says.[6] "They had no intention of being a hearing [aid] company," she recounts, but when she screened emails from a hundred thousand people on the company's waiting list for mentions of any type of hearing issue, she learned that 25 percent wanted to use the new earbuds for this purpose. She said, "that's your goal. You have a market here," and signed on to help build the product.

Apple beat Doppler Labs to market with its wireless earbuds, and the startup could not raise the capital to continue its operations. It closed in 2017.[7] But Liu had talked with legislators in the US Congress about updating the law regulating hearing aids as medical devices to expand access to the market for technology companies. A new law was enacted that year. Prescription hearing aids cost $2,000 or more. Liu was thirty-nine and estimated she had spent $60,000 over her life so far replacing broken ones. "I win a big part of that conversation because I am able to walk in and say look, I'm not just a technology company trying to make money, I'm someone who has been deeply affected by this my entire life, and here's technology that could change people's lives and give them access," she says.[8] In 2022 the Food and Drug Administration issued regulations to implement the law, authorizing the sale of hearing aids to people with low to moderate hearing loss without a prescription. They cost as little as $200.[9] The market for the technology is now estimated to be larger than $1 billion.[10]

Financial Data

Financial data includes information about sales, revenues, investments, expenses, acquisitions, divestitures, and profits. The finance department is an obvious source for financial data, but you can also find information in sales, procurement, mergers, and acquisitions, and from any manager with profit and loss (P&L) responsibility. Consider these:

- the revenue each product or service produces, and how profitable each product or service line is
- how sales teams or individual salespeople perform
- revenue from each channel, office, or region
- how much each of the organization's revenue streams contributes to its growth
- how each unit manages its expenses
- customer acquisition and retention costs
- how much the organization spends with its suppliers and in what areas
- investments the organization makes in startups, partnerships, or joint ventures
- mergers, acquisitions, divestitures, or spinoffs

Companies usually know how much revenue individual salespeople bring in, and which business units (and managers) are best at managing expenses. They may also know which customer segments spend the most, or what their highest-spending customers buy. But many companies do not dig deeper to connect the demographics of their workforce to revenues, cost control, profits, or growth.

Data about the millions of dollars that companies spend on contracts is another underused source of information about diversity, equity, and inclusion. Even when companies have programs to diversify their suppliers, they may report only aggregate numbers. Segmenting this data can reveal how the organization distributes supplier contracts: whether, for instance (as John Rogers at the University of Chicago observed), racial and ethnic minorities mainly provide labor but not advisory services, technology, or product components. When you segment demographic data on your investments in startups, joint ventures, mergers, and acquisitions, you can learn whether you are investing in firms that serve demographics you do not, or that are owned and run by people who are underrepresented at your organization. By studying the data on businesses you plan to sell or spin off, you can find out whether these have a disproportionate impact on under-represented stakeholders.

PepsiCo under Indra Nooyi, its first female CEO, transformed its product portfolio, reformulated popular products, and expanded its investment in what it calls "better for you" and "good for you" foods. The strategy was driven by alarming trends in public health. The company—known for its sugary drinks and fatty, salty snack foods—had to make its products healthier because to do otherwise made it complicit in customers' premature deaths from obesity, Nooyi argued. Though investors were initially skeptical, the company's revenue during her twelve years at the helm nearly doubled, from $35 billion to $64 billion. By the time Nooyi stepped down in 2018, the healthier offerings represented about half of PepsiCo's products worldwide.

Having leaders who share the perspective of core customers has been essential to PepsiCo generating profits, says Umran Beba, who retired from the company in 2020 as senior vice president and chief global diversity and engagement officer. For example, three out of four food and beverage shoppers worldwide are women. "When I joined the company in 1995, we were focusing a lot on youth," says Beba.[11] "And if you mention PepsiCo to a general consumer, they might say, 'Oh it's a youth brand.'" (Ad campaigns for Pepsi's soda brands target young consumers and often feature children and pop culture celebrities.) However, as she points out, in a fragmented and global market, the company could not survive without products that adult women want to buy.

With this insight, the company's diversity, equity, and inclusion efforts included a focus on appointing more women to sales, supply chain, and general management roles where they would "immediately be affecting the revenue and the profit and then making sure that they are part of the agenda building this company to the next level," according to Beba. As of 2022, women held 44 percent of management roles at PepsiCo—up from 37 percent in 2015—and 40 percent of executive roles. The company notes, however, that "manufacturing remains male-dominated, partially due to societal bias, workplace culture and physical demands of roles," and that gender parity in operational management lags that of corporate management.[12]

Paula Santilli, the PepsiCo CEO for Latin America, explains how she measures the contributions of women from the factory floor to the executive team, demonstrating repeatedly that diverse teams get better results. For example, sales teams staffed and run by women consistently beat sales targets and lose less money to fraud. "So, we're giving opportunity to women in sales like never before," Santilli says.[13]

Operations Data
Operations data includes information about how the organization executes its business processes. This data can be highly industry and organization specific: a manufacturing company operates differently than a bank or a retailer, while nonprofits, startups, and small private businesses operate differently than large public companies. But whatever they do, organizations keep similar types of data:

- delivery time, including how long it takes to deliver a product or service and whether it is delivered in the time frame promised
- safety, including accidents, security incidents, and illness outbreaks
- product and service quality, including errors
- waste
- shipping metrics
- returns and refunds

When combined with employee, customer, or financial data, operations data can tell you where your best, most productive performers are, as well as whether your operations deliver the same level of service to all of your customers. In recent years many organizations have also studied their operations with an eye toward accommodating remote work. Data can highlight whether some groups of employees are at risk of being excluded from career opportunities because they don't come to the office every day. For some individuals with health concerns, the potential for exposure to infectious disease is a safety issue, observes John Danley, an aerospace industry executive, while parents may decide their families are better off if they work from home, and younger workers may simply prefer it.[14]

Santilli, the PepsiCo executive, points out that manufacturing lines in Mexico staffed only with women have been more productive and made fewer errors. "Because we compensate on productivity, they make more per hour. A few months into this, and the men next door were saying they wouldn't mind getting a few of these women onto their line as well."[15]

When you have data, you can identify changes you can make to your operations that improve outcomes—both for your organization and for its people. I know a middle manager who leads safety and security for a global cleaning products manufacturer. One of his responsibilities is to provide training for employees in how to protect themselves from physical threats. The company operates in South Africa, where car theft rates are high and thieves are aggressive. They have dragged people, even babies, from occupied vehicles. The manager had to develop special training for employees to respond to this threat even when driving their own vehicles. He had served in the military and observed that women and men face distinct threats and respond to them differently, including that mothers may put themselves at greater risk when protecting their children. Knowing this and knowing that employees included many women with children, he created a program tailored for them. He used heavy-duty vehicles that were harder to handle than passenger cars and taught women how to maneuver them aggressively but safely. He included a lesson about what to do if their children were with them.

External Data

External data includes any information produced outside of your business that is used to make decisions. Many organizations use external data to benchmark their operations and performance and to understand customer, industry, and employment trends broadly. It can come from a variety of sources, including industry associations, market and public opinion research companies, government agencies, universities, think tanks, and social media platforms.

As with customer data, a variety of departments including HR, sales, marketing, finance, manufacturing, procurement, and strategic planning may collect external data:

- independent market research, including market share data and forecasts
- consumer trends
- public opinion surveys about social, political, financial, and business topics
- industry trends
- government data on population, household finance, employment, industry concentration, and economic growth
- competitor data
- social media data about your organization, market, or industry (which may overlap with customer data)

Some of the most useful types of external data for diversity, equity, and inclusion cover the demographics of your organization's market. This data can show how well your organization is positioned among different demographic groups as well as provide fodder for discussion about opportunities for future growth. In the Fortune 500 bank that I mentioned earlier, an all-White executive team led the business banking division, and it did not see any need to address diversity. These division leaders were satisfied with their revenue, which they knew came from a predominantly White customer base. But they changed their minds when a new diversity, equity, and inclusion advisor showed them market data about the demand for business services from non-White executives. With information about the opportunity to compete in markets they had been ignoring, the bank created two new business segments to serve these customers and appointed Black and Hispanic executives to run them.

The Right Metrics

Having the data is only the beginning. Unless you can show that your efforts to include more diverse leaders and managers are, in fact, resulting in more diverse leaders being appointed, and that they are making the organization better in ways leaders think are important, it will be easier for everyone to revert to old ways when their initial enthusiasm for diversity, equity, and inclusion has subsided.

"You have to have the metrics, and then you build the roadmap for improving on those metrics and results," advises Tracey Gray-Walker, the AVMA Trust CEO and former chief diversity officer.[16] "Additionally, you have to be transparent and acknowledge that you can't impact everything simultaneously. Using a systematic approach improves the chances of success." What you measure, and what you include on your scorecard or dashboard, will depend on your business strategy and what your executives care about. You can't measure everything.

If you are just starting out, you will want to focus on what matters to your executives most and connect your diversity, equity, and inclusion goals with those key business goals. If you choose the right two or three metrics, you will prompt questions that potentially lead to more metrics. Before you begin, it's important to understand where your organization will have the opportunities to appoint leaders to achieve the goal and when these roles will be open or created. You can't create roles out of thin air or without a business rationale. Next, determine the percentage of talent that is available internally for promotion and over what time frame. Are people ready now, or will it take six months, a year, two years, or more? Do you intend to promote only from within? Third, you will want data on the talent available externally at the levels where you are focused.

You may already do this analysis at an aggregate level. To add the dimension of diversity, you will need to segment your employee data to understand the gaps in leadership, as well as in your internal and external pipeline, between the majority and the groups that are underrepresented. From there you can develop near-term or aspirational goals for the diversity traits that are needed in leadership and management. The organization will work toward these percentages over a defined period.

Finally, you will choose a few metrics to track your progress toward these goals and their connection to a business goal. Let's imagine your customer base is becoming more ethnically and racially diverse. You plan to pursue growth in these new segments, but most of the leaders and managers at the company are in the ethnic majority. You know from your research that the demographics of your current workforce overall are similar to the demographics of your expected customer base, so you set your goals for developing your pipeline accordingly.

Your scorecard could include these measures: the availability of talent among underrepresented groups, their levels in the organization, and their rate of appointment to open positions. Each department or function may take a different path to reach the goal based on whether they have opportunities to hire or promote anyone. But the scorecard will show leaders how far they have progressed and where they need to go.

Metrics can also point leaders and managers toward actions they might take to make progress. For example, if the organization uses employee engagement surveys to monitor job satisfaction, it can segment the results by demographic groups to learn whether people in underrepresented groups are as satisfied as those in the majority. If people leaders correlate these results to employee turnover metrics and track these numbers over time, they can see whether their diversity, equity, and inclusion efforts are improving the work environment and opportunities for all employees. If the organization can collect data in its surveys about what may be causing dissatisfaction, it will have evidence to justify changes to its career advancement or workplace policies. In addition, the data can reinforce the value of policies and practices that are helping the organization meet its retention goals.

At Baxter Healthcare, our senior leaders wanted to improve retention among women who were leaving the company to take leadership roles elsewhere. Baxter had a reputation for developing high-caliber leaders, especially CEOs, and our people were in demand. Retention had become a key business objective because the company was restructuring. We were going to lose people as we eliminated jobs, but we needed the high-potential talent we had invested in to stay. We didn't want them walking out the door because they could not envision a career with us.

When we dug into our demographics, we learned that many fewer women than men were being appointed to director or vice president roles, which meant they would not become eligible for more senior positions. More importantly, we could see where women were getting stuck. We learned, for example, that there were no women in P&L roles. With the data in hand, we convened focus groups of women and men in areas of the business where high-potential women were not advancing to hear about their experiences in the organization. We learned from these conversations that women lacked role models who resembled them, and that to be noticed they had to behave like the men. Many women and men alike lacked awareness of their current skills and those they needed to succeed because managers did not spend time on career development. Instead, they said, advancement was driven by "politics" and relationships developed informally. Women more often lacked exposure to the leaders and managers who assigned development opportunities.

We took action to improve those areas, targeting these and other barriers that the groups identified. For example, we set a goal for improving the overall business culture, as measured by scores on our employee survey. And we created a guide for leaders that pinpointed the decisions, behaviors, and specific actions that would enable us to make progress.

To address the imbalances for women, we established two goals for female representation in leadership that we aspired to achieve within three years: one for the director level, and another for vice president and above. These were based on our expectations for the number of openings that we would have in this time frame, as well as the availability of women in our internal pipeline and externally in our industry who we could consider for these positions.

Further, we asked people managers to ensure they invested in developing high-potential talent. Specifically, we advised them to provide opportunities for women to interact and work with senior leaders. We also asked them to be aware of the transferable skills that people on their teams could develop, and to coach these. Because transferable skills enable people to succeed in roles they do not have direct experience with—such as a product manager becoming an operations leader—we told managers to assess these when making hiring and promotion decisions.

Within a year we increased the representation of women at the vice president level by 2 percent. We used data to shine a spotlight on the specific areas where women were overlooked, took steps to increase their visibility to decision-makers, and tracked our progress using a dashboard and a scorecard. I worked with our global head of leadership development and our head of talent analytics; we presented our progress quarterly to the senior executive team and reported to the board twice a year.

Questions to Define Objectives and Outcomes with Data

When you have data, you can illuminate both the opportunities for including a more diverse group of people on your leadership teams and what has been holding them back. From there, you can establish concrete goals and metrics to measure your progress on what matters to your organization most. Start with the end in mind. Choose a business priority to focus on, assemble some relevant data, and answer these questions about it to get started:

- What is the demographic representation of my current and immediate future stakeholders? What does this show me about the diversity I need among my direct reports and in my organization?
- What data do our senior leaders and the board of directors discuss regularly that they can review through the lens of diversity, equity, and inclusion?
- What does my data show about the business opportunities we are missing?
- Considering the mix of diversity traits on my team, which of them will make a difference to what I must deliver for the organization?
- What does my data show about how different segments of my team and the workforce feel about their managers, jobs, and career prospects?
- What does my data show about which segments of my team or the workforce are less likely to advance into leadership?
- What does my data show about the demographic composition of our leadership team and pipeline?
- What does my data show about how my direct reports are investing in building and developing the leadership and management pipeline?

II Using the ABCD Framework

6 How to Use the ABCD Framework to Break Down Barriers

In earlier chapters I've encouraged you to ask a question when you think about the leaders you need for your business: Who is missing? Now I will show you how to harness the power of this question to drive solutions for identifying, developing, and retaining a greater diversity of leaders, whether they come from among the talented people already in your ranks or you are hiring them.

You will not get a list of programs to implement here, as I said at the beginning of this book. What you do will depend on your circumstances. I cannot know which solutions will work for you. Rather, as has been the case throughout this book, I'll give you a foundation for thinking about the levers you can pull and some principles to help you succeed. These are the same levers and principles I've used throughout my entire diversity, equity, and inclusion career. Although the examples I share from my work or leaders I have interviewed are not prescriptions, I hope they spark ideas or validate your efforts so far.

As we've covered, a wide range of humanity is well represented in staff and lower management positions in many organizations.[1] It is not similarly represented in senior management because existing leadership development practices and corporate culture have put up barriers to some people's advancement. When you remove them, many more potential leaders will become visible. The barriers tend to fall into a few broad categories:

- People who differ from the majority are invisible to leaders and managers when they look at their customers and their workforce.
- The process for identifying potential leaders leans more on managers' personal opinions than an evaluation of individuals' character traits and behaviors.

- Managers do not spend enough time with their direct reports to learn about their goals, understand their potential, identify their development needs, or give them useful feedback.

- Individuals with leadership potential do not get the assignments they need to develop their skills and abilities or increase their exposure to the colleagues and customers who influence whether they advance.

- People lack role models for how to succeed and informal opportunities to build relationships within their organizations and their industry.

Changing how your organization identifies and develops leaders requires a deliberate and sustained effort. Inertia tends to rule. If leaders and managers think current practices work because they find qualified people to fill open positions—even if they keep choosing people from the same group—they may not see any incentive to change. It may also be true that many managers, especially middle managers, aren't empowered to change how they make personnel decisions, even if they want to. They will need to be—and to be held accountable for the results. These are the people leaders who largely determine who does what work and who becomes visible to senior management. They choose team leaders, hand out stretch assignments, give performance feedback, and decide who gets promoted. They also serve as gatekeepers to informal opportunities for their team members to meet people across the organization who will influence their career paths.

The specific barriers, and how to remove them, will be different for every organization and may be different for groups of people within it. This will quickly become clear if your organization operates in more than one country or region. Or if it chooses the people it develops for leadership from a limited range of departments, such as finance or marketing, but never research and development. Meanwhile, some barriers that we associate with one group may affect everyone. Flexible schedules help all parents navigate the demands of work and child-rearing, though people frequently think of them as a benefit to women.

Every person, whatever their differences, will need information, encouragement, training, experience, and support that is tailored to them. Not everyone experiences the workplace alike or has the same understanding about the career paths that are open to them. Some people, including people in the majority, will not think of themselves as leaders until a manager who sees their potential plants the seed.

I am an example. If it weren't for my boss Wendy Jean at Sodexo, I wouldn't have become a diversity, equity, and inclusion leader. I enjoyed my marketing job. When my friend Elaine, an internal executive recruiter, suggested I apply to be a director in the company's new diversity, equity, and inclusion department, I turned her down twice. I didn't even understand what the new position was about. Wendy Jean chimed in—she told me I would be great at it. I still wasn't interested. But when Elaine came back a third time, I agreed to put my name in, if only so she would leave me alone. When I got the offer, I still didn't think I wanted it. But I needed a job; our marketing team was being disbanded. And it changed my life. From the first day, I felt I was doing what I was born for. I have felt this way every day for over two decades. If it weren't for my friend and my boss, who both saw something in me I didn't, I might never have known.

If we expect managers to define their jobs as orchestrating work, rather than nurturing talent, they may place no importance on helping people discover their ambitions and develop their abilities, especially if they are being rewarded only for managing to business results. When organizations focus solely on efficiency and productivity, managing to the numbers becomes a higher priority than investing in people. Managers may think that ambitious leaders will identify themselves and ask for opportunities. If this is the philosophy of the organization, and if on top of this there is no formal career path, managers have little incentive to dedicate time to developing anyone. They may think they have fulfilled their responsibility if the organization offers training, even if it doesn't get results.[2] Anyone who leads people should be involved in clearing away the barriers to development for their employees—all of them—and creating new systems, processes, and cultural norms that encourage people with leadership potential to discover and pursue it. This requires a long-term commitment, as I have said. As with any corporate commitment, it will need a guide and champion: in this case, a dedicated, business-savvy diversity, equity, and inclusion leader.

Organizations need a leader in this role who people leaders think of as a trusted advisor. Appointing someone who is not solely an advocate for a moral or legal position but is a member of the team working toward common business goals is a critical step toward repositioning diversity, equity, and inclusion from an administrative, charitable, and compliance-focused function to one that is embedded in how the organization runs its business. Organizations do not select their business or function leaders based on perceived moral or legal obligations, nor do they select them based on visible characteristics such as ethnicity, gender, or race. They should choose a diversity, equity, and inclusion leader just as they would any other leader.

The absence of such a leader is often a barrier. Let's look into that first.

Appoint a Business-Savvy Diversity, Equity, and Inclusion Leader

As I've noted, many C-level leaders still see diversity, equity, and inclusion as separate from how they run their businesses day-to-day, even when they fervently believe that more diversity in leadership is a worthy goal. This is because promoting workforce diversity and making the workplace more welcoming to all have been defined, managed, and led as an administrative and compliance function. Managing employee and race relations, advocating for equal opportunity, counseling and training employees, and investigating discrimination complaints are necessary (and will continue to be so). But they are support activities that are disconnected from anything that generates revenue, serves customers and clients, or fulfills a mission. Even though many organizations see HR as a strategic business function, they may not yet see diversity, equity, and inclusion as an essential component of their business strategy. Diversity, equity, and inclusion leaders, meanwhile, may be passionate about their mission. But if they define it solely as advocating for underrepresented groups or as a charitable endeavor, rather than making the organization more successful, they will struggle to be effective. Fortunately, advocacy for people and for the business go together because, remember, you can't run a business without people.

Tracey Gray-Walker, the insurance executive, served for five years as the senior vice president and chief diversity officer with AXA in the United States. Although as an accountant and business leader she had never worked in HR, she had run client management, strategy, and operations for a business unit focused on retail customers, and she had led teams of various sizes. Senior leaders knew her reputation as "a full-immersion learner" who got results. "It was a very heavy lift," she recalls, and it challenged her skills at creating relationships with her colleagues.[3] "I learned to assess what landed well, and what did not. I also spent a fair amount of time working to collaborate with my colleagues with a focus on meeting them where they were."

She reflects that as a "tall, broad-shouldered Black woman," it was more difficult to connect with the company's White male leaders than it would have been for someone who looked like them. "You just have to get people comfortable with who you are first before you can even get to the work," she says. Her business knowledge and experience created common ground with many leaders in the company. "I understood what the goals were, I was numerate, I put metrics around everything we did." Business leaders "are always looking for KPIs, and always looking for bottom line impact," she continues. If you speak the language of numbers, "you can align them around some of the work you're doing, because that is what resonates with them. It is all about the results."

Choose a Leader Who Can Influence

A few years ago, Korn Ferry, a leadership development consultancy, defined a profile for a "best-in-class" chief diversity officer. The study concluded that the most effective diversity leaders are sociable team players who are motivated to collaborate with others. They're good at managing conflict, persuading people, and behaving courageously when having difficult conversations. Most diversity, equity, and inclusion executives did not fit the profile.[4] They were, strikingly, unlikely to be driven by opportunities to collaborate.

A colleague once shared his frustration about his lack of progress after only one year in the role. He was particularly unhappy that he was not getting the data he needed from HR to build his plan and scorecard. He was preparing to meet with the company board of directors, and he intended to end his presentation by asking for their help. When I probed for more information, he shared he had never met with the head of HR to discuss the matter, he had not built relationships with the needed partners, and his supervisor was not aware he was going to raise his problem with the board. I advised him about an alternative path. But my colleague's initial approach is unfortunately common. It's no wonder that so many diversity, equity, and inclusion executives struggle, then leave for other organizations, perhaps before they have any results to show for their efforts. Denise Hamilton, a consultant, points out that diversity, equity, and inclusion officers may have a shorter tenure, on average, than other executives—three years, versus five for CFOs—because their companies lose enthusiasm for change.[5]

There is little question, as well, that diversity, equity, and inclusion leaders are expected to respond to every crisis of discrimination and inequity. It's an exhaustive list: mental health, sexual politics, religious rights, racial, ethnic, and gender conflict, remote work policies, court decisions, and immigration are only some issues. They are also expected to be strategists, trainers, coaches, advisors, negotiators, communications experts, therapists, and much more. Both the workload and the emotional toll are heavy. We can see evidence of this in the data on chief diversity officer appointments. A study of the S&P 500 by the HR advisory firm Russell Reynolds noted a twenty-five-percentage-point increase in these positions between 2018 and 2022. At the same time, average tenure in them has declined because of a combination of "concern for the personal demands placed on CDOs," a lack of business support, and lack of resources.[6]

But I'll argue that because many of these leaders aren't well suited to the requirements of the role, the deck is stacked for frustration and stagnation. Systemic change is unsustainable without strong, business-focused leadership and the skills to influence decision-makers. Executives and managers across the business become distrustful when they do not see progress, and they respond as they do whenever they are not getting a return on their investment. They cut resources when budgets become tight and revert to familiar practices that they view as having been successful in the past.

Some organizations have elevated the chief diversity, equity, and inclusion officer to a C-level position, which gives the person in this role an opportunity to contribute directly to top management decisions. A top management title can also signal to employees and the world at large that diversity, equity, and inclusion has equivalent status to other business functions. But I think it's more important that this leader, wherever they are on the organizational chart, has the right personality profile and competencies. As Richard Taylor, the Nasdaq employee experience leader, puts it, "While we can all see the obvious positional authority that comes from a big title, I'm sure we all know C-suite leaders who are not particularly influential. I think influence is a choice, and a skill, and absolutely anyone in any role can be persuasive and influential."[7]

Taylor reports to Nasdaq's chief people officer, which puts him one step below top management and provides some positional authority. However, he considers the following traits, which are associated with people, not titles, as the keys to influencing business leaders: "Do you demonstrate empathy and care for others? Do you express a clear vision of a better future where everyone can see themselves in the picture? Are you good with setting clear goals and measuring progress rigorously? Do you bring colleagues at every level along with you? Do you build lasting, trusted relationships, from the CEO to the individual contributor?"[8]

People with these traits can inspire followers anywhere in an organization. And inspiring followers is part of the essence of good leadership. As Marcus Buckingham and Ashley Goodall write in their book *Nine Lies about Work*, "What distinguishes the best team leaders from the rest is their ability to meet these two categories of need for the people on their teams. . . . Firstly, that you make us feel part of something bigger, that you show us what we are doing together is important, and meaningful, and secondly, that you make us feel that you can see us and connect to us and challenge us in a way that recognizes who we are as individuals."[9]

If your organization already has a diversity, equity, and inclusion leader like this in place (or you are that leader), it is on its way. If not, it will want to find one, and then give this leader a team and resources to support their work. It must invest in them the way it would any essential business function—starting with creating a full-time role. Too often, organizations ask someone—usually from an underrepresented group—who already has a full-time role to take on this work without compensation. But they can't be effective as a diversity, equity, and inclusion leader if they are being paid for doing something else, even if they are an eager volunteer.

The diversity, equity, and inclusion team will be responsible for vision, strategy, coordination, and guidance. But the investment will extend beyond it. Every business unit, department, and function will contribute to creating and implementing more inclusive decision-making systems, policies, and practices. The middle managers leading these teams will assign analysts to delve into their business data, include images featuring a diverse range of people on organizational websites and in marketing campaigns, survey customers, educate their leaders and workforce, and more.

Sixteen years ago, when I was at Rockwell Collins, the marketing, communications, philanthropy, and talent acquisition teams financed the creation of an advertisement by the agency Mintz & Hoke that showed some of our equipment and the diversity of our workforce. The ad was so brilliantly done that it became the image the company used for its brand advertising at the Paris Air Show (the world's largest trade fair for the aerospace industry), in the Cedar Rapids airport, and in magazines for a decade. I didn't have a single dollar for this in my budget. But as the diversity, equity, and inclusion leader, I had influence. I commissioned it to help solve a business problem.

Figure 6.1

Rockwell Collins's diversity, equity, and inclusion function did not have an advertising budget. It collaborated with marketing, communications, philanthropy, and talent acquisition to produce a 2007 ad showcasing the diversity of the company's workforce and products. Image © Collins Aerospace.

Remove the Barriers to Advancement

When you remove the barriers to advancement for talented and qualified employees who are not in the majority, you help to create a diverse bench of potential leaders and managers. This bench has three legs:

- Opportunity, in the form of open roles for which talented employees with diverse characteristics, life experiences, and abilities can be considered.
- An internal pipeline that reflects the diversity of the workforce of leaders and managers who will be ready for greater leadership.
- An external pipeline of potential hires for leadership and management roles that reflects the broad diversity of the world.

Let's begin with opportunity. As I have said before, talent is abundant, but opportunity is not. Organizations have blind spots, just as individuals do, because they comprise people who created the formal and informal systems, processes, and policies by which they operate. The barriers to including more diverse leaders and managers that I listed at the beginning of this chapter are some of these blind spots. They prevent talented and qualified leaders, and potential leaders, from being noticed and chosen for increasingly bigger roles.

To remove the barriers to opportunity, you first have to identify them. When diversity, equity, and inclusion leaders, together with business leaders and their HR partners, use sound assessment methods for selection, development, and succession planning; assess potential as distinct from performance; delve into business and workforce data; and gather information from employees about their experiences at work, they will uncover the specific obstacles that make people who differ from the majority invisible. When I say that people are *invisible*, I mean that the individuals deciding whom to appoint to leadership and management literally don't see them because they have not met them, learned about their talents and accomplishments, or seen them in action. It's difficult to imagine anyone in a leadership role unless you know them.

To address this issue at Baker McKenzie, I conceived a program to sponsor high-potential women partners. Leaders Investing for Tomorrow (LIFT) pairs these women with senior leaders, who spend a year advising them on their career path and helping them to build the skills and experience to advance within the firm. Two years after launching the program, most women who had taken part in LIFT were running an office or a practice. This is due significantly to the visibility they gained with those senior leaders.

"That planted a seed that, hey, my firm definitely sees a future with me," says Stephanie Vaccari, who heads the Intellectual Property Tech Practice Group in Toronto, Canada.[10] She was nominated for the first LIFT cohort in 2017, just as she was exploring her future career path with the firm. She requested—and was paired with—a sponsor who was also a member of the firm's executive committee. This executive "was instrumental in directing me and expanding the people that I know," Vaccari continues. "Prior to LIFT, a lot of my visibility was only in the IP group." By participating, Vaccari could also present her work to other leaders. "I was able to showcase what I could offer. Putting stuff on paper is one thing but having these decision-makers in front of me, listening to what I do, and what my practice is, and what I can offer, is a completely different thing." Two years later, Vaccari was appointed the first female managing partner in the Toronto office.

When we choose people for our teams or recommend people to our colleagues, we are likely to focus on those we have worked with closely or who are part of our professional or social networks. The higher we rise in the leadership ranks, the more likely we are to be surrounded by people who are like us. Unless you already have a network full of people who are not like you, you have to be deliberate about including candidates who represent the range of people in your organization, industry, community, and even the world when you are filling any position. However, many leaders still say they don't know where to look for a diverse slate or how to evaluate people whose experience they haven't shared.

Even when we have a diverse network of relationships and sources for talent, filling a key role can take months. We think about how quickly we can get someone into it and up to speed, and not about taking more time to learn about the people in our organizations who are ready to be leaders but whom we or our close colleagues don't already know. Under pressure, we're also unlikely to reconsider our ideas about who is qualified and who is ready. We end up deciding based on preconceived ideas about the type of person who is a good "fit," even if we set out to consider candidates who are not from the dominant group.

Every manager can put structures in place to counteract their deeply ingrained assumptions about what leadership talent looks like, sounds like, and acts like. I know a manager who is part of a research team at a US university that recently received a $2 million grant. The application guidelines encouraged applicants to partner with universities that primarily serve students from underserved populations in the United States and with researchers at those institutions who could advance knowledge about the needs and barriers that underserved populations face. As the team was strategizing, members raised a critical issue: they didn't have connections with these institutions. The discussion prompted the team to identify a new partner who had relationships in the communities that needed to be included. I'll also point out that the team members, including the manager, were not making the final decision about whom to include, but they had influence—as can anyone, if the environment supports them.

Many people still harbor stereotypes about people who differ from them, and they may need to examine their own assumptions about who makes a good leader. A study published in 2019 by the IBM Institute for Business Value and Oxford Economics shows how persistent some myths can be. Researchers surveyed over 2,300 executives and professionals—including an equal number of women and men—to learn about the barriers to women in leadership. Respondents' explanations for why there weren't more female leaders included assumptions that fewer women than men were interested in leadership roles and that women were more likely than men to choose their families over their careers.[11] Although these observations tend to be true on the surface, if you dig into why, it's not that women don't want to be leaders so much as that they lack role models and support to pursue these positions. The IBM study found that respondents were almost twice as likely to say women sought raises and promotions to the same extent as men if their companies were investing in them.

Education about these kinds of biases can prompt us to be more aware of how we think about and interact with people who are not like us and to confront stereotypes. It can help us recognize when we are letting our preconceived ideas influence our decisions, rather than the facts in front of us. But we do not need training to ask ourselves and our colleagues who is missing from the rooms where we make decisions and use our curiosity to understand why (for example, by using the Five Whys method of exploring problems). Once we understand why, we can begin removing obstacles and help talented people from every group reach the highest levels of leadership at the same rate.

> We do not need training to ask ourselves and our colleagues who is missing from the rooms where we make decisions and use our curiosity to understand why.

Data helps us to see. Remember that many organizations think about their customers, as well as their workforce, in aggregate without exploring whether different segments have distinct wants or needs. Your efforts to align diversity, equity, and inclusion with your organization's business priorities will illuminate opportunities to improve and grow by creating more diverse leadership and point you to areas that need attention. When you segment your workforce by demographic characteristics and by role, you can see where the leaders you need are in your pipeline and where they are getting stuck.

Many organizations have this data but haven't looked at it. If you do not have it, you can begin to collect it. And you can start asking questions. For instance, you may notice a statistically significant difference in the rate women are advancing compared to men, or Black people compared to White, Hispanic, or Asian people. Digging further into data such as retention rates, employee satisfaction, and access to development opportunities can help to illuminate the reasons.

Don't overlook ingrained social behaviors that may prevent all people from thriving. These are barriers, too. A corporate culture in which leaders use sports analogies for everything, or that expects everyone to wear a polo shirt (offered in limited sizes) and a baseball cap for a company event instead of providing a choice of attire, is a culture that perpetuates exclusion of anyone who is not familiar with sports or who feels uncomfortable or unattractive in those clothes. It's a cliché because it's all too often what people experience.

Listen, and People Will Tell You the Truth

Whether or not you have quantitative data, you can also understand a lot about the barriers to opportunity through conversations with leaders, managers, employees, customers, and other stakeholders. An outcome of building strong partnerships with stakeholders is honest dialogue. Who you talk with will depend on your role and the people you have access to. A diversity, equity, and inclusion leader can facilitate these conversations and share the results across the organization. But if you ask anyone what is holding back segments of the workforce who are underrepresented in leadership and management, they will tell you, in detail, about their experiences. Talk to enough people, and you will see common threads.

After George Floyd was murdered, a lot of CEOs and board directors began talking with each other and their employees about what happened. These conversations led to discussions about how different groups of people were responding to the news, and, further, how they felt in the workplace. Some leaders learned for the first time that some groups were having negative work experiences. A senior leader in a global executive search firm told me he had no idea his Black colleagues and employees were having unacceptable experiences until he held listening sessions with them in 2020 after Floyd's murder. This surprised him because his experience in the company had been one of openness, comfort, and kindness. "We are a great firm and I thought everyone was having the same experience I was having," he said.

These conversations may also produce stories, like the ones in this book, that can help to personalize the effects of certain behavior or practices on different groups of people. Leaders may sincerely wonder why they don't see more diversity in their ranks but not take further steps to examine their organizational culture. Stories about what people in their workforce have experienced can prompt them.

At Baker McKenzie, an employee survey revealed, to no one's surprise, that both female and male attorneys wanted more flexible work arrangements. In focus groups, women described being excluded from opportunities to take part in the social life of the firm—an essential way for attorneys to develop relationships with leaders who can influence their careers—because some events took place away from the office, in the evenings, or on weekends. When I shared this finding, one executive recognized his own behavior. He not only changed when he scheduled his own informal gatherings, but he began holding them at the office. The results were almost immediate. During one of the first in-office gatherings, he talked with a female member of his team who shared her career aspirations. Though he worked with her, it was the first time he had learned anything about her vision for herself. And he went about setting up what she needed to achieve her goals.

Rethink the Leadership Pipeline—Inside and Out

Of course, not all barriers are that easy to eliminate. The employee survey we did at Baker McKenzie told us that the structure of middle management and senior roles discouraged women from participating. These barriers had nothing to do with their level of experience, their effectiveness at creating good client relationships, their productivity, or their success at bringing in revenue. The women were discouraged by workplace norms, including a lack of flexibility about face time and working hours, and an absence of role models.

For instance, the firm had an intense meeting culture. Attorneys were expected to attend in person, which required constant travel. As part of its action plan, the firm implemented a flexible work-life policy. This enabled each office around the world to establish the practices that were relevant for them, including endorsing remote attendance at meetings when attending in person wasn't feasible. The new policy contributed to an increase in the percentage of women promoted to partner by over 50 percent within a couple of years. Because men at the firm also struggled with balancing life and the demands of being a lawyer, endorsing a flexible work-life policy helped everyone.

You will not have a bench of qualified leaders at the top of the organization unless you create it from the bottom and the middle. "If you want a pipeline, you have to build it," observes Taylor, the Nasdaq leader. "Customers don't fall into your lap. Profits don't fall into your lap. A diverse pipeline will not fall into your lap. You're going to have to go earn it."[12] Commit to doing it, and you can make significant changes quickly. It does not have to take years to see progress.

Tackle the Pipeline from the Top

It is oversimplifying only a little to say that some obstacles can be banished by will, and that the actions of senior leaders can set a powerful example.

Diversifying the board of directors is one way that organizations can show progress while setting up to make deeper changes. There are plenty of people representing a vast variety of identities and abilities who are qualified to sit on corporate boards; it's only that they may move in different circles than the people doing the appointing. Those people only need to look beyond their existing networks. Recall that Robert McDonald, as chairman and CEO of Procter & Gamble, decided his board needed more women. All that was left to do was ask them to join.

Similar logic applies to appointing executives to the levels directly below the C-suite and the leadership teams within business units or functions.

When you look for leaders outside of your immediate circle, you can find qualified candidates representing every identity.

Gray-Walker, who serves on several corporate boards, observes that directors can help management connect diversity, equity, and inclusion to business strategy by asking the right questions. These are some areas where boards might focus their attention:

- ensuring the organization invests in the success of people who are newly hired or promoted
- monitoring whether the organization consistently offers competitive compensation, professional development opportunities, and career advancement
- confirming that every team applies the organization's talent management processes and that inclusion permeates these processes
- defining the diversity goals the organization aspires to, how long will it take to achieve them, and how progress will be monitored

With these actions, boards can help to institutionalize diversity, equity, and inclusion. They prompt changes to how everyone in the organization thinks and behaves when hiring, developing, and promoting talent. Boards can also push for commitments from top management and hold leaders accountable for following through on them.

When I was at Baxter, we were not concerned only about appointing women as leaders and managers. Black people were not represented in these roles, either. I did an exercise with our senior leaders to define their circle of influence—the people they knew who they could rely on to step into a leadership role. I called it their personal influence network (PIN). You can do this exercise if you are hiring at any level. They drew concentric circles, putting their family members and closest friends in the center; the people they knew from the country club, places of worship, boards they sit on, and other institutions in the middle circle; and loose relationships with people they knew from work or home (such as friends of friends and former colleagues) outside of that. One executive, upon completing his circle, saw that he had one Black person in his middle circle he could recruit for the position they needed to fill. Without going through the exercise, the executive would not have identified this person who was a good candidate for the leadership team because he wasn't connected to the people the executive spent the most time with.

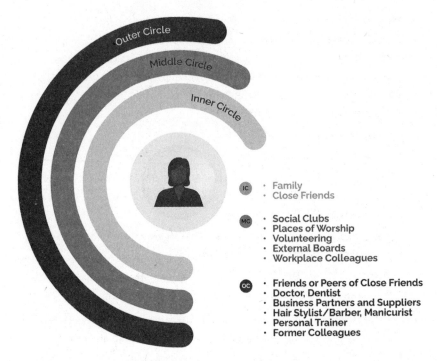

Figure 6.2
A personal influence network provides a graphic representation that can help leaders and managers identify a wider range of people to consider when filling open positions in their organizations.

Senior leaders can also eliminate barriers in the executive recruitment process by holding search firms accountable for presenting more diverse slates of candidates. Here's another example from my work at Baxter. When our CIO left, we had another opportunity to appoint a Black executive if we could find the right candidate. The human resources vice president directed the head of leadership development and talent, who was in charge of the process, to have the search firm include Black people on the interview slate. When the first interview slate had none, the vice president pushed back. When the second slate of candidates still had no Black representation, and the reason given by the search firm was that they couldn't find any, the vice president demanded more. Finally, the third slate included Black candidates. We hired the best qualified individual. He was Black. He held the role for almost ten years and was beloved. He became a member of the C-suite because his leadership was so valuable to the company. And we would not have found him if our HR vice president had not insisted our search firm look beyond their usual sources.

Build the Pipeline Inside and Out

An equitable hiring process is essential to finding the best candidate for any role. Whether they are recruiting from inside or outside the organization, hiring managers can insist that searches include a final interview slate of candidates with different backgrounds, experiences, and abilities. This can be a simple conversation—almost a check-in. For example, during a business update, a colleague who was hiring for my team shared where they were in the hiring process for a newly created intern role. I said, "Describe the diversity of the final interview slate." He gave me a robust response that highlighted the outreach and screening he did to ensure he had a diverse slate from which we could make our choice.

Specifying that the final interview slate address the gaps in representation that you want to close is critical. Otherwise, stakeholders will propose candidates only to have them fall out during the process because they aren't qualified. It's a way for recruiters and hiring managers to say they've tried without making an effort to find people who are suitable for the role and have potential to make it to the final round.

Nasdaq is creating a more inclusive pipeline internally in part by revamping a leadership development program for high-potential employees. Previously, the company invited ten people annually to participate, all of whom were candidates for appointment to vice president. "It was very prestigious and exclusive, and diversity wasn't a factor at all," recounts Taylor.[13] The new program, which costs less, is open to a hundred midcareer employees (a level where there is greater diversity in the workforce). Vice presidents nominate participants from across the company who equitably represent the geographic, gender, racial, and ethnic diversity of the workforce as well as the diversity of business departments. By targeting a larger, more diverse talent pool at a lower level in the organization, more people who are more representative of the workforce can gain experience that they need to advance and exposure to people who will choose them. "We believe [it] produces better networking opportunities for participants and better builds a pipeline of leaders for the future who really understand our business," says Taylor.

Leticia Gonçalves, one of the women appointed to lead a region at Monsanto, took over a team that was 100 percent male and did not reflect the diversity of backgrounds and nationalities in the twenty-nine-country region. When she did, she recalls, "I made significant changes to increase diversity and inclusion from background, nationality, and type of leadership. I changed my marketing lead, I changed my product supply lead, I changed my supply chain lead, to really bring new thinking and bring other kinds of experiences that we didn't have in the team before."[14]

Gonçalves had identified several women internally with the potential to advance further. But they needed time and experience to be ready. Even then, there weren't enough of them to bring a critical mass of women—30 to 40 percent—to the top levels of leadership in the region. "We created a project to start hiring females into deeper levels of the organization to make sure we were building that bench strength for future years," Gonçalves says. Meanwhile, she took steps to address her need in the short term by recruiting externally.

If you plan, you can create an external bench that can supplement (or complement) your internal one. A few years earlier, under the directive of Michael Frank, the international operations leader at Monsanto, I worked with his business and HR leaders to build an external bench while we worked on the internal one. We took an approach similar to that of executive search firms by building relationships with women across the industry who were talented and might be open to joining the company in the future. This network was available to Gonçalves and anyone else who was hiring to fill a leadership or management role in Europe. No one could say they didn't consider any women because they couldn't find any who were qualified.

Although Monsanto was acquired, and Gonçalves left before she could see the outcome of all her efforts, the point remains that she could not immediately get the full range of perspective and experience she needed by choosing from the array of leaders in front of her. Only by casting a wider and more inclusive net was she able to find the leaders that she needed to get the results she was after.

Make All People Leaders Responsible

The involvement of the Nasdaq vice presidents in nominating a more diverse slate of candidates for development highlights another critical underpinning of efforts to include people who are missing: the role of each people leader. Who middle managers decide should prepare for bigger roles, and whom they appoint, depends on what the organization expects them to do and the support they get. A first step is to define people leaders' responsibility for specific diversity, equity, and inclusion outcomes; what they are expected to do; and how they will be supported and evaluated—just as for any other objectives.

Organizations can include progress toward these outcomes in managers' KPIs. These may include, depending on a manager's role, check-ins with direct reports, performance reviews, talent calibration meetings, and town hall meetings. The KPIs can include expectations for behavior that supports inclusion. Then, what managers have done to develop and advance people with experiences that are underrepresented in leadership and management can be weighed along with their other contributions when they are evaluated. Any performance goals you set for individual managers need to connect with the aims of the organization. The behavior you expect from them needs to be defined concretely. And the criteria you use to evaluate them, as well as the outcomes for achieving or falling short, must be clear.

You should apply the same level of accountability that you have in place for any other goal. If managers succeed, you can reward them. If they struggle, you can delve into why, and provide support to overcome any obstacles. If they persistently fail, they should not have opportunities to advance to bigger roles themselves. In extreme cases, you might need to remove them from a supervisory role, even though it's challenging to do so. This is because they lack the capabilities to succeed or help the organization in a talent development position.

And here is the key: every manager should have the information, education, and tools to get the job done. Then they should get a reasonable amount of time and the coaching they need to succeed. People become experts in their fields through formal education, internships or apprenticeships, certifications, and years of on-the-job training. Yet many leaders and managers do not get any preparation to lead people. Meanwhile, most of them have minimal understanding of diversity, equity, and inclusion, or of how to lead with that lens in mind. So it is crucial to set them up for success.

Julie Eaton, a former DuPont executive, recounts that for many years, business results were the only criteria she had to evaluate her direct reports. She had no approved metrics to encourage behavior that would keep her

teams motivated, engaged in their work, and feeling as if what they did mat-
tered. Several years ago, however, the company articulated a set of behaviors with which it aimed to redefine the culture. These included making an
impact, acting like an owner, and partnering with customers. The business
goal driving this change, says Eaton, was to attract and retain diverse talent
and create an environment where employees "could see themselves in [an]
exciting future with opportunities to grow."[15]

Employees got examples of what to do, as well as of what they shouldn't
do. "Innately, I would have wanted to measure those things. But had I made
those up in the past and held my people accountable to a set of metrics
that didn't exist for everyone, it would have completely backfired," Eaton
says. "Now I could say, here are your business results, and when I look at
make an impact, act like an owner, and partner with customers, this is
what they mean for our part of the business, and this is what I'm going to
hold you accountable to. We included diversity and inclusion, and what it
looked like."

Eaton had examples to counter "some of those statements people make,
like 'she's not ready.'" Eaton could point to "the behaviors and the capabilities that we need in a job." She could prompt managers to examine what
they had done to develop those capabilities in the people on their teams
and see who was, in fact, ready to advance. "We articulated things that
were important to us as a company, that we believed were important to our
customers, and that everyone could do, so that breaks down some barriers,"
she adds. Individuals, regardless of their gender, race, ethnicity, or other
inherent characteristics, might practice those behaviors or capabilities differently and still "be consistent with who we are as an engaged and inspired
organization."

Empower People Leaders to Act

When I talked to Eaton, one detail in her story struck me especially. As a
middle manager, she could not decide on her own how to evaluate the
people on her team. It wasn't until the company gave her metrics to assess
how employees behaved that she had permission to manage and develop
her team in a way that she knew would get better results.

Consider that every company has Julie Eatons—leaders and managers
who understand that the character and values that team members display

are as important to business performance as their skills, but who do not have a framework for acting on these instincts. Consider also that there may be leaders and managers who are unaware that they behave in ways that deny some of their team members opportunities to contribute to their utmost ability. If they are made aware and advised on what to do differently, they can change their approach.

Defining a talent development model for leadership—the behaviors and capabilities that leaders in your organization need to master along with their skills and experience—can even empower managers to make decisions that they may have once felt were risky. Think about an organization (maybe your own) whose current leaders are mostly White men with MBAs from top-tier schools. Absent guidance that defines leadership behaviors and capabilities, a middle manager who is choosing an account team leader to promote to sales director might think it safest to choose another White man with an Ivy League degree because he is like the other leaders, even if he has only the minimum qualifications. The Latina with an MBA from a public university who leads a high-performing account team, who solves problems creatively with her team members, and who consistently reaches out to colleagues who can help her is more likely to be seen as ready, and to be chosen, if her manager knows that these are essential behaviors for company leaders. The manager knows, because the criteria make clear, that her race and the university she attended should not count against her.

Suppose this Latina account team leader has only been in the role for a year. She might not be a contender for sales director yet. In that case, her manager, recognizing her potential, will understand that she needs opportunities that will help her get to the next level and beyond. Remember Mark Mendez, the attorney at Davis Polk, who advocated for junior attorneys to work on transactions that would help them gain experience they needed to advance. And as we saw with Best Buy, a one-on-one discussion with a manager can be a powerful tool for understanding employees' capabilities and what they each need to reach their potential. Managers who do not provide team members with the attention and support they need to succeed can be yet another barrier. Says Taylor:

> You can't just say, "Oh, well, Susan has never had experience in accounting." OK, did you give Susan an opportunity where she could build up her accounting experience? I've also had leaders say, "I've got this wonderful woman in my succession

plan, but she's about three years away from being ready." Well, the next year, she's also three years away from being ready, and the year after, she's still three years away. So, I have to kind of call their bluff and say, "Well, what are you doing with Susan? Is she getting speaking assignments? Is she going to conferences and presenting, and is she leading a really visible project?" Oh, she doesn't have the financial acumen. "So, what are you doing to get her the financial acumen?"[16]

Not every high-potential employee will articulate their ambitions. I never did, even though I've always been very ambitious. Most of my managers told me only what was wrong with me. Once, after a presentation, my supervisor passed along feedback from another executive saying that I was "too polished," as if this was a bad thing. But she could not explain what this feedback meant or explain what I was supposed to do about it. This happened years ago, but employers still rate people using stereotypes and do not offer useful advice. Research by Textio, a vendor of talent acquisition and performance management software, found that Whites are most likely to be described as "easy to work with," women tend to be described as collaborative and helpful, and men are more likely to be deemed confident and ambitious. The same survey found that women, Blacks, Hispanics, and people over forty are least likely to receive actionable feedback.[17] In my career over more than three decades, only three managers invested in my development. A conversation in which a manager highlights an employee's potential can awaken ambition in someone who is talented but has not been encouraged. Or, like my conversation with my boss Wendy Jean at Sodexo, it can validate the ambition in someone who needs to know they have an ally to help them define their path.

There can be cultural reasons that make it risky for people who are not members of the majority to express their goals, and personal reasons that make people hold themselves back if no one encourages them. I have coached and advised many exceptional leaders who have held themselves back.

It isn't news to anyone that the behavior of women in male-dominated settings is interpreted differently than that of men. Hispanic women have shared with me that their friendliness and enthusiasm—which is part of their culture—is often assumed to be flirtatious. Women who engage in behaviors associated with good leaders—being assertive and confident—may be seen as selfish or abrasive, while Black women may be perceived as angry.[18] Black men who do the same in White-dominated settings may be viewed as arrogant or threatening.[19] "You don't want to be the threatening angry black man, so portraying that jolly side, that happy side, that optimistic side weighs heavily," says Milton Davenport, the Chicago endodontist. "Professionally, it does help to present yourself a certain way—or at least it did. I think it's getting a bit better with my son's generation. But with something like an endodontic career, it's all about short-term relationships. I would say you have a very short period of time to make a good impression on someone, for them to trust you enough to jab a needle before a root canal."[20] Organizations need to address these cultural barriers, too.

And some people will become interested in leading only when they are presented with the opportunity. Jami McKeon, the Morgan Lewis chair, did not aspire to the role. "The honest truth is that I never made the decision that I wanted this job until I was asked to take it," she says.[21] But from the beginning she gravitated to opportunities to be involved in what she calls the life of the firm. "So, if people asked me to be on the cafeteria committee, sure. The recruiting committee, absolutely . . . it was very organic." Over time, by serving on firm-wide committees (including one that decided partner compensation and a board that advised the firm chair), she gained exposure to senior leaders. "There were several people who put me in positions of opportunity to develop leadership skills to influence people around me and to be well positioned for a role that I had not thought about wanting or taking," she says. "I think, to the degree that it was a foregone conclusion that I would do it, it was only because of that long history of having been at a firm where I wanted to be engaged and felt not just included, but responsible, and part of the ownership of the firm. It would have been very hard for me to say no."

Here's another beautiful example of the difference active encouragement can make. Many years ago, at Google, executives observed that female engineers did not apply for promotions at the same rate as men. As reported in the *Washington Post*, the senior vice president for people operations was familiar with research showing girls do not raise their hands in math class, nor do women contribute ideas in business meetings, as often as boys or men. He concluded that the same behavior was in play when it came to applying for promotions and tried an experiment. When the head of an engineering group in the company emailed his entire team reminding them to apply for promotion and citing the studies, more women applied for promotions and their promotion rate rose. One time when he forgot to send the email, the rate of female applicants fell. The women, as the Google executive put it in the news article, needed a nudge. And Google delivered it in a way that included everyone.[22]

This solution is so brilliantly simple that any company can implement it or something similar. All they need to start is to acknowledge that people have different ways of understanding their potential and advocating for themselves and to help managers learn to reach them in different ways. When you remove the barriers—individual and organizational blind spots—that make it more difficult for people from some groups, or easier for others, to become leaders, you will gain a view of the full breadth of talent available to your business.

Questions for Using the ABCD Framework to Break Down Barriers

A business-savvy diversity, equity, and inclusion leader will be able to guide other business leaders through the organization's data, policies, and practices and reveal who is getting stuck and why. By working together, leaders and managers at every level of the organization can change how they identify and develop future leaders so that everyone with the talent and ambition to lead has the opportunity to pursue their career goals. A well-resourced diversity, equity, and inclusion function that is positioned as essential to achieving business goals can deliver lasting benefits to an organization by ensuring it develops and retains the talent it needs to do so.

The following questions will get you started:

- Do we have a diversity, equity, and inclusion leader who is well versed in how the business makes money, the customers it serves, and the markets where it operates? Does this leader collaborate and build relationships well?

- Where are people from underrepresented groups advancing at significantly slower rates than people from the majority?

- What do my data and my conversations with leaders, managers, employees, and other stakeholders reveal about the barriers to including more people from underrepresented groups in leadership?

- How does my organization determine who has leadership potential?

- What is the quality of the feedback I'm giving? Is it clear and actionable? Do I focus on team members' personalities more than their performance?

- How do managers choose which people get assignments where they can acquire skills and abilities they will need for bigger roles?
- Am I attuned to the range of motivations and identities of the people on my team that lead to unique development needs?
- Do leaders and managers know why diversity, equity, and inclusion are important to the organization and what their responsibilities are in helping to achieve them?
- Have we given managers the training, tools, encouragement, and permission they need to change how they evaluate people on their teams for their leadership capabilities?

7   How to Become an Inclusive People Leader

Leaders and managers create and reinforce the business culture, and they create the opportunities for employees to learn and grow. This is why organizations need inclusive people leaders. But if we are going to lead more inclusively, we must first pause and inspect where our worldviews come from—particularly what we believe about who belongs and who doesn't. In our daily lives, we are so busy doing, planning, leading, teaching, coaching, consulting, even being chefs and chauffeurs that we may not make time for introspection and learning. When we do, we begin to understand that we have no control over many factors that shape our views, such as our heritage, our families, the country where we were born, and our skin color.

These factors lead to our biases—which, again, we all have. When we become aware of them, we can start to notice how they creep into our behavior and decisions that either include or exclude others. And when we see them, we can choose to change. We can close the gaps between what we say we value and our actions, becoming more effective people leaders in the process.

We become inclusive by reflecting on how we as individuals show up for the people who are following us, whether these are employees, customers, business partners, or members of the communities where we work. Do we behave toward everyone in a way that is consistent with the values of our organization? Does each person on our team always feel comfortable contributing to the work? Or do we treat some team members as insiders while leaving others out?

My aim in this chapter is to give you the tools to raise your personal awareness and prompt you to action. We are all starting at different points on this journey. Inclusive people leaders are constantly observing and learning. I invite you to begin by being curious and courageous, becoming aware of your blind spots, committing to change, and being collaborative with your people. These are the traits of inclusive cultures that I introduced in chapter 4. Here, I want you to look inward, to examine your own daily behavior and interactions with people. No one becomes an expert in anything without effort. It takes years of experience and education to gain wisdom in our chosen discipline, and we continue to learn. Learning to be inclusive is no different. We're on a continuum from unknowing to knowing to action. But each one of us has the power.

Be Curious

The more I travel, read, and listen, the more I realize what I don't know—and that I can't know it all. Consider a few things that we may not know about the people on our teams, simply because we have projected our thoughts and experiences on them instead of being curious about what they are thinking and experiencing:

- If we are used to speaking up and being listened to, we may not know that some of our colleagues are struggling to be heard.
- If we feel free to talk about our families, we may not know that some of our LGBTQ+ colleagues pretend not to have families rather than risk rejection or attack.
- If we are native English speakers, we may not know that it can be difficult for non-native speakers to understand us. We may talk too fast or use words that do not have equivalents in their language. Even if they speak fluently, they may be translating in their heads, which is exhausting.
- If our sacred days never fall on workdays, we may not know that our colleagues have to choose between attending a client meeting or observing a religious holiday.

One way you can apply curiosity is to observe whether the same people are usually silent during your meetings and ask them why. Listen to what they say—you may not like the answer—and explore with them what they need to make their voices heard. If you have included them in the meeting, they have something to contribute. Remember Michael Frank, the Monsanto executive, who was missing insight from the introvert on his team because he assumed that if she had something to say, she would speak up.

Trait	Inclusive culture practices	What leaders do
Curious 	Encouraging people to ask questions of themselves and others about processes and decisions that affect the team, its work, and the business.	When they observe people speaking or behaving differently than they expect, they explore the reasons why.
Aware 	Exploring what our teams, and our organizations, are missing about people who are different from ourselves, or from the majority, so we can see our blind spots.	Take note of their assumptions about people who are different from them and what they are missing about the individuals on their teams.
Courageous 	Making it safe to discuss a broad array of subjects, including seemingly unpopular ones; to make unconventional choices, and to experiment.	Be open to having potentially uncomfortable conversations, listen without judgment, and change how they behave toward others based on what they learn.
Committed 	Agreeing the company will inspect and update its systems, processes, policies, and practices to make them more inclusive.	Continuously reflect on how they lead their teams and act when they identify practices and behavior—whether their own or that of teammates—that should change.
Collaborative 	Individuals working effectively with their team, peers, and partners to discover what inspires and motivates them and helps them achieve their goals.	Learn what inspires and motivates each person on their team, and their goals; make all team members feel included by giving each one support and attention.

Figure 7.1

The traits of inclusive, welcoming cultures align with the behavior of inclusive people leaders.

When we are curious, we open ourselves to other people, and we can see how we are different and alike. The CEO of a technology startup told me that during a tense team meeting, a female colleague became frustrated and cried. Later, a male employee shared his dismay at her emotional outburst. The CEO pointed out that this employee had let loose a series of expletives because he was also frustrated. When the employee explained his reasoning, the CEO calmly asked, "But isn't your outburst an emotion, the same as hers?" By being curious, and asking a question, the CEO was able to coach the employee to greater understanding.

Be Aware

There is an award-winning video from Coca-Cola that I often share in my workshops that exposes our tendency to judge people based on scant information. Six strangers, all men, sit around a table in the dark. As they talk to each other about their interests and expertise, they also share what they think each person looks like. When the lights come on, they see how wrong they were. A man who reads deeply about psychology and has given a TED Talk is imagined to look "nerdy." He is covered in body art, which another man admits he would have found threatening if he had seen him in the street. The group is surprised to see an extreme sports athlete in a wheelchair.[1] Once, after I shared this video, a financial services executive revealed his blind spot: that he struggles to hire people with body art because he knows clients will push back. Others will share their biases about the food people eat, the music they like, their accents, where they went to school, the clothing they wear, or the skills they have (such as those of non-engineers in an engineering company).

Outside of a workshop or an experiment, we have many opportunities to take note of our biases if we are open to doing so and we are paying attention. You might connect a story you hear on the news with a comment from a colleague or a customer. Or a conversation with your daughter, a partner, or a friend who is frustrated at being passed over for a promotion might make you curious whether people in your organization who are like them feel similarly about their careers.

Remember that how we interpret the world, how we see other people, and even how we perceive ourselves is a function of our experiences, education, and the images and messages that wash over us daily about who is normal, desirable, and belongs, and who is different, undesirable, or "not one of us." We lean on these beliefs to decide in an instant whether we can trust someone based on their appearance, how they move, and how they speak. This means we're guaranteed to misjudge people, often without being aware that we're doing it.

Be Courageous

Before we become aware of our limited understanding, we may deflect and even deny the realities of others because this information does not align with what we thought. Instead, I invite you to reflect on the wisdom of Joan Chittister, a Benedictine nun and author, who advises us to see our limitations as a gift to ourselves. "If we refuse to ask for help, if we distance ourselves from the strengths of others, if we cling to the myths of authority and power where trust is needed, we leave out a piece of life," she writes. "It is trust in the limits of the self that makes us open and it is trust in the gifts of others that makes us secure."[2]

This takes courage. You take the chance to be open and trust in the gifts of others when you listen to outsiders' voices and believe the stories you hear. These are not ridiculous, far-fetched, or invented to seek attention. They're simply different from your story and those of the people who raised you, grew up with you, went to school with you, live next door to you, or worship with you. When you find yourself discounting information that does not conform to your worldview, practice asking yourself: What don't I know about this that I should? Have I considered I could be wrong?

Bruce Boyd, the advisor to philanthropists, reflects that his life experiences so far—including volunteer work as a young man tutoring low-income students in a violence-ridden neighborhood, traveling the world as a tourist and for work, and owning a small farm with his family in a rural part of his state—have made him sensitive to and appreciative of differences. But they have not been enough to make him, a White man raised in an affluent suburb, an inclusive people leader. "I've had some very good guides and mentors along the way," he says: people who differ from him and will tell him "when I might say something or do something that wasn't as inclusive as they believed I aspire to be."[3] He continues, "My hope is that we have open and honest conversations and we each bring value to the conversation in different ways. In an ideal situation, you as a leader promote conversation that is open, honest, and authentic, and people feel free and comfortable in that sort of environment."

Many of us tend to avoid such conversations. It takes courage to confront someone about behavior that has hurt us or others. In a survey by Crucial Learning, 51 percent of respondents estimated they put off engaging a colleague about their performance or their treatment of people for at least a week.[4] Muster your courage and follow where your questions and observations lead you. You could start by writing down the stereotypes you have of people and cultures and make an inventory of those things. Where did they come from, and how did you learn them? From family members? At school? Or did you soak up these views because they are pervasive in society and you breathed them in with the air? Which ones are you perpetuating, practicing, or preaching? Then work on them, one at a time, by noticing when a bias or stereotype may be influencing your behavior and learning how to behave differently.

Be Committed

To be committed is to continuously self-reflect. This is an ongoing, never-ending endeavor. Then you should turn your newfound awareness into action. It is possible, for instance, that the financial services executive from my workshop who has an aversion to body art is wrong about his customers. If he asks them about it, he might learn that they do not have that bias. The larger question for him is where he draws the line. If he cannot commit to including on his team a talented leader with body art, how committed will he be to including others who some customers may deem unsuitable because they have physical disabilities, or are out as LGBTQ+, or have some other visible difference? To be an inclusive people leader he has to show he can give everyone an opportunity, regardless of their characteristics.

Milton Davenport, the Chicago endodontist, notes that patients are sometimes upset to hear Spanish speakers on his staff conversing in their native language. "It's really offensive to people to hear someone speak in Spanish when they don't understand Spanish," he observes.[5] He understands where the attitude comes from, having grown up at a time when political leaders insisted immigrants should not be accommodated if they couldn't speak English. Davenport has turned that approach on its head. "When they're speaking in Spanish, I'm trying to learn Spanish, so this is great for me," he says. "I don't have the patience to coddle that mindset, that you're just so stuck, that they have to be like you. That's their native tongue. That's the way they learned how to speak. That's where they feel comfortable. Why should they have to switch the way they speak" when they are talking to each other? His decision to let employees be themselves and to make the effort to learn their language shows his commitment to being inclusive.

Be Collaborative

Every leader has power, though its details vary. But anywhere in their organization, inclusive people leaders can use their power to bring outsiders in rather than forcing them to fight their way through. When they do, they develop collaborative relationships with their people. We can exercise our power on three levels: when we interact with individuals, when we lead meetings internally or interact with our stakeholders, and when we make decisions about people, systems, policies, and processes.

One-on-one, we can build trusted relationships with people by showing that we are interested in them and care about them as human beings. I am not suggesting you pry into anyone's personal life. We should respect each other's boundaries and abide by the laws that protect our privacy. But many people routinely share details of their lives outside of work with their colleagues. They may keep photos of family members or a memorable trip on their desks. They may hang a poster of a favorite print on the wall. These are invitations to dialogue. The same goes for stories they tell about their travels; experiences they had growing up; a gadget they bought; the movie, concert, or game they saw over the weekend; or the restaurant meal they enjoyed. Observe, listen, and be curious. Ask to know more, as you would to show anyone that you care about them. If the person responds—and especially if you discover common interests—you have the basis for deeper understanding.

Michael Santa Maria, the Baker McKenzie practice leader, relates that in every conversation he has with his team members and clients, he talks

> Anywhere in their organization, inclusive people leaders can use their power to bring outsiders in rather than forcing them to fight their way through.

about his family and asks them about theirs. "You cannot talk to me for thirty minutes without knowing about my family," he says.[6] By sharing his values and inviting others to do the same, he's able to sense and address the issues they uniquely face in terms of their gender, role, family status, race, tenure, language, culture, and other differences. Because he sees the whole individual and what is getting in their way, he can take steps to clear those obstacles. He can change his own behavior and leadership style if that is the issue or lead the charge to change a policy or process. When he does, he shows each person on his team that he values them and cares that they succeed.

He describes one associate with potential to run the firm. "I realized after having worked with her for a couple of years that she innately has a commercial, pragmatic sense that is beyond her years of work. I think that was part of her upbringing because her mom ran a business in Colombia. . . . I don't know either of her parents, but we talked about both of them a lot. She gets her business sense from her mom, so, that's one thing that she brought to the table that we're working with." Santa Maria learned this about the associate's background and connected it to her abilities because he showed an interest in knowing her as a person. You won't learn what drives people, how they came about their worldviews, or anything else about what makes them tick during a business meeting or when you're troubleshooting a problem with a client or a project. You are also unlikely to uncover the struggles or stresses in their personal lives that might affect their ability to succeed at work. Santa Maria clarifies, "Not that I can demand of them to have a successful life, but the expectation is that they're going to put the time and effort into it, that it will be successful, and it's not 'come to work at the expense of your life.' Because as an employer, you never win that trade in the long term."

When we engage with our teams, our customers, and other stakeholders to understand people's life experiences, we can take further steps to ensure that we are collaborating with each person. This helps ensure that we do not separate people into insiders and outsiders and give only the insiders our support and attention.

Keep in mind these seven ways we can make people into insiders:

- Speak up for people who are not in the room and represent the perspectives of the people who are affected by a decision.

- Involve people in decisions that affect their jobs or work environment.
- Notice when people are not participating in discussions and find out why.
- Let other people in meetings share their views first rather than staking out your position at the start and listen to them actively.
- Ask advice from a variety of people rather than the same people each time.
- Facilitate discussion to ensure teammates listen to each other's ideas and inspect them rather than passing judgment on them instantly.
- Advocate for more inclusive systems, policies, and practices in the organization that will help team members succeed.

A story from John Danley, the aerospace executive, illustrates the power that collaborative leaders have to model inclusion on multiple levels. Several years ago, when Danley was a department head, a member of his team approached him for a private conversation, during which the male-presenting employee disclosed a desire to transition socially and professionally to living as a woman. The employee felt comfortable telling Danley before contacting HR "just because of your demeanor."[7] Danley was unfamiliar with the gender transition process, and the company had no policies for supporting transgender people. But he didn't hesitate. "I said, we're going to treat you equitably."

After working with his employee and HR to collect research and advice about how to proceed, Danley brought the team together and communicated his support for her. He acknowledged that some team members might feel uncomfortable (though he was comfortable), but he expected that she would be treated fairly and her career would not suffer. He observed that the world was changing, and they had to respond. He also welcomed being the first team in the company to have the experience. "And I think most of the organization adapted and changed as well," he says. "They saw the individual transition in front of their eyes. And it was, I think, a beautiful thing."

Here's what I want you to take away from this story. A team member trusted Danley enough to share an important decision about her life and identity—one that would for a time affect her performance and had potential to change her relationship with her team. Although the issue was new to Danley, he listened, asked questions, and helped. He helped her navigate corporate policies, helped protect her career opportunities, helped her teammates accept her, continued to include her as a valued colleague, supported her if she encountered obstacles at work, and helped the company evolve its policies.

Contrast this story with another that I have adapted from my work. The behavior described isn't unique to any organization. After a lengthy search for a new procurement director, a manufacturing company hired an employee named Ono from a leading competitor. At a team meeting shortly after their start date, Ono suggested a new way to approach collecting requirements from the product teams. Their manager, who led the meeting, commented, "That's a very interesting approach, but here we collect requirements using our tried-and-true method and the results feed nicely into our system for evaluating proposals." No one else spoke up. Here, the company had put enormous effort into hiring someone from elsewhere who could provide fresh ideas, and yet their manager communicated, in front of the entire team, that their ideas were not welcome. By invoking "how we do things," the manager in effect defined Ono as an outsider for thinking differently.

Ono's manager demonstrated none of the five traits of inclusive people leaders that I outlined earlier. He seemed unaware of his bias in favor of business as usual; rather, he treated it as a settled fact. He showed no curiosity about Ono's idea, which may have required courage to explore. Though he had presumably hired Ono because he wanted their perspective, he wasn't committed to exploring it. And he took no steps toward collaborating with Ono as a partner during that meeting.

Here is another way the manager could have responded: "Thank you for that idea, Ono. One reason I brought you on this team is for your perspective on our processes and how we might improve them. Let's plan to meet soon to talk about this more." The manager not only would have communicated that Ono is a valued member of the team—an insider—but also would have signaled his openness to hearing about new ideas from others.

I would also like you to notice that all we know about Ono from this story is that they are a new employee. As I've said throughout this book, diversity and difference extends beyond the characteristics of people we can easily see or hear. When you are an inclusive people leader, you work on practicing inclusive behavior every day, in every encounter, with everyone.

When we become practiced at including everyone, we can see more readily, as Danley did, how to treat each person equitably and use our power as people leaders to do so. We begin to speak up for the people whose voices and perspectives are not being heard because they are not in the room. We begin to collaborate with our colleagues to change the systems, policies, and practices that have turned some people into outsiders. We become advocates for each person on our team. And we earn their trust.

Inclusion Creates Trust

You are not an effective team because you work together but because you trust, respect, and care for each other. If leaders and managers do not trust their people, and people do not trust their leaders, they limit what they can accomplish together. But how we build trust with others depends on how they approach it themselves.

Some people will trust us right away, but we can lose their trust over time. Others won't trust us until we earn it. Either way, whether we lose trust or earn it depends on how we behave toward another person. A Black employee once told me that she used to value HR but lost trust after turning to her White HR manager for help. The manager intimated to the employee that she didn't believe her story and therefore did nothing to solve the problem. The employee lost faith and never sought help from the HR manager again.

In *The Speed of Trust,* Stephen Covey writes that trust begins with personal credibility. You need to show integrity, your motives need to be clear, you need the means to accomplish what you intend to do, and you need to be able to get results. Covey goes on to describe a set of behaviors for building trust that are similar to the behaviors of inclusive people leaders: listening, showing respect and care for others, showing loyalty (by recognizing others' contributions and speaking up for them), engaging in tough conversations, and what Covey considers "the quickest way to build trust in any relationship": making and keeping commitments.[8]

"If someone was not performing, they knew I would cut them," says Maria Boulden, the former DuPont sales director.

> They also had the trust to know if I was bringing someone in, that person deserved to be there. People know immediately if you are structuring for politics, for demographics, or some other reason other than I want the strongest, most successful team possible. Everybody knows it, whether they talk about it or not.
>
> So, early on, if you can establish, as a leader, that your primary purpose and mission is to make this team the best anybody's ever seen, they will feel it, they

will trust it, and they will execute accordingly. That opens the doors for the people you bring in, even people who seemingly would have been looked at as someone who doesn't belong, whether they're young or old or, again, from a different region or gender-wise different.[9]

When employees trust their leaders, they are more engaged, more productive, and less likely to quit. Why? Because when we trust someone, we feel safe with them. When we feel safe, we are more likely to offer our ideas and share our unique viewpoints. We become empowered because we are not afraid of being ostracized if we express ourselves. When we trust someone, we will trade with them. We will share information about our background, career aspirations, and what is getting in the way of us being productive and efficient. But we will not feel safe or empowered or trusting unless we feel that we belong. We won't get all the benefits of greater diversity until we can trust each other. So we need to practice inclusion to create trust.

Think about your inner circle again and make a list of the five people on your team you trust the most to advise you. Are they like you in generation, nationality, gender, ethnicity, and native language? If they are more like you than not, you aren't only limiting your access to information that could lead to better decisions. You are also sending a message to everyone on your team that unless they resemble you, they are outsiders and you do not trust them. Ask yourself why, then, they should trust you and give you their best. A participant in one of my workshops was practically giddy during this exercise because it revealed her blind spot: the reason she was having such a difficult time leading her organization was that she trusted no one.

Next, consider who the insiders and outsiders are on your team and who is missing. There's a simple way to tell. The insiders have input into what the team does and the way work is done. You consult them while you're making plans and before you make decisions. They speak often in your meetings, you welcome their feedback, you address their needs, and you give them opportunities to learn, grow, and advance. Many insiders also tend to be long-tenured, to have more resources, and to have greater access to unique information and networks at higher levels of the organization. The outsiders are the people whose input you dismiss or do not seek, whose voices you do not hear, whose needs you do not consider, and who do not get the same opportunities. They feel they cannot count on you, and you have to earn their trust. Many people—leaders, managers, and employees alike—have shared with me that when they have been outsiders, they felt like failures or foreigners. Some feel hopeless, ashamed, or unfit. Others describe loneliness, anxiety, and feeling neglected. Many of them said they were just acting on the job.

Ask and listen. No matter the context, people want to be listened to and become frustrated when their ideas and perspectives are neither considered nor sought. Many of us can recall an experience in which we were not consulted about something that affected us, or, if we were, what we said was ignored. Listening is widely considered an important behavior for effective leadership, yet a survey of four thousand employees in eleven countries by the Workforce Institute at UKG and Workplace Intelligence found 63 percent feel their "voice has been ignored in some way by their manager or employer," while 34 percent would rather quit or change teams than tell management what they think about their work environment. Thirty percent reported they are heard the least on "diversity, equity, inclusion, and belonging initiatives."[10]

There may be many reasons why some people leaders struggle to listen. Furthermore, we process information and make decisions exceedingly fast. We make instantaneous judgments about whether the information we're getting is useful, and we may miss the significance of what someone is telling us if we're not paying close attention.[11] But people leaders frequently tell me they anticipate it will be difficult to act when employees raise concerns about inclusion, so they avoid these conversations. Most of the time, though, employees are realistic; they know leaders won't be able to do everything they ask for, all the time. They only want to know that their ideas and perspectives are being considered, and to have an honest conversation. You can be open to listening while being truthful about what you are able to do.

You can turn outsiders into insiders. Some steps may be easier than you think because you can execute them within your team. In your one-on-one meetings, you can listen more than you talk—and then decide with your employee what steps you will take to help them with their concerns and their growth.

When you know what your team members need, you can be mindful of it when you run your meetings. If people are translating what you say into their native language as they listen, you can speak in a simple way that makes this task easier. When team members are visually or aurally impaired, or who are visual or aural learners, you can consider different ways for them to access the information they need. You can provide meeting agendas in advance to give team members preparation time.

When you add people to your team, you can invite current members to contribute their ideas about whose perspectives they need. They may uncover your blind spots. When you create new products, plans, policies, or processes, you can ask for ideas and feedback from people who are representative of the population who will be using them, or who will be affected by them.

If your team is global, you can have representation from team members in each region when you are planning work and setting deadlines to create a common understanding about what will be done and the process for doing it. Otherwise, you risk wasting time, money, and effort. I know a trainer at a global technology company who invested an enormous amount of time in designing a training that he was going to deliver around the world. In India he spoke for an hour and a half to a rapt audience that nodded throughout. He felt confident and successful until it was over, and he asked for questions and feedback. That's when they told him they struggled to understand what he was teaching them. They were nodding because in their culture this was a way to show politeness—not agreement or understanding. If he had included someone on this team to give him cultural insight, he would have learned how to judge whether this audience was comprehending his presentation and how to adjust it. Instead, he wasted the time of everyone involved and cost the company money. He felt embarrassed and lost confidence in himself.

Whatever steps you take, note the results. Do you have closer relationships with more people? Have you learned information about team members that you did not know before and that helps you to lead them? Has the quality and timeliness of your team's work improved? Are you pursuing new ideas that make your group more productive or your organization more efficient and profitable?

Questions for Becoming an Inclusive People Leader

Begin your journey with the conviction that being inclusive will make you a better people leader, manager, and colleague, and that your team will do better, too. Staying the course requires courage, strength, and determination. But people who commit to inclusion do so because these objectives align with their corporate (and perhaps their personal) values, and because they believe it is good for their business.

To start on the path to becoming an inclusive people leader, ask yourself these questions:

- What is a story, a moment, or an experience from my life that changed the way I view the world?
- Am I willing to change my mind when the facts contradict my prior beliefs?
- Am I aware of how social inequities show up within my area and affect my peers' or team members' experiences?
- When I lead meetings, whether they are in person, virtual, or hybrid, do I give everyone an opportunity to participate and ensure they are not interrupted? Do I favor certain people or groups during our team discussions?
- How often do I ask, What do you think?
- During a meeting, do I allow people a minute or two of silence to think about what we are discussing?
- Do I understand the individual and collective needs of my employees? Are they telling me what they need? Do they feel comfortable expressing any concerns or issues about the work environment?
- Which inclusive behaviors are most important to helping my team achieve our goals?

8 A Call to Action for Diversity, Equity, and Inclusion in Leadership

Many people start out thinking that diversity, equity, and inclusion is a program with a beginning and an end, that at some point, we will achieve our goals for a fair and equitable workplace—and society—and can invest our time and resources elsewhere. I welcome your idealism. But we should be realists. As much progress as we make, the work of diversity, equity, and inclusion can never be finished, any more than the work of growing a company can be. The world, and the people in it, are constantly changing. Unless we become hermits, we will spend our lives encountering situations we have never experienced, and people whose languages, cultures, and values are different from any we've known. We can't predict what will challenge our beliefs or what we think we know in the future.

We could not know, for instance, that a worldwide pandemic in 2020 would drive more women than men from the workforce, often because they lacked childcare; that it would reveal to some that people don't need to work in the same physical space to be productive; or that millions of us who accepted going to the office day after day would find life without a commute so much less stressful and more fulfilling. And we could not know that, because of these trends, organizations would rethink how they manage people to continue to attract and retain talent.

Nor have we solved the problems of discrimination because of bigotry based on religion, race, ethnicity, gender, sexual identity, and many other differences, even though we have been working at this for centuries. Around the world, we find people becoming less free.

Meanwhile, environmental, social, and governance risks are increasing. As the World Economic Forum notes in its *Global Risks Report 2023*, "Mounting citizen frustration at losses in human development and declining social mobility, together with a widening gap in values and equality, are

Diversity is a fact. Inclusion is an act.

posing an existential challenge to political systems around the world."[1] The risks from climate change also threaten the lives and economic security of people around the world. We are likely to see more people migrating from homes affected by war, economic crises, extreme weather, and habitat loss to places where they can survive and be safe but will be outsiders.

We don't have to look far, in fact, to see that in-groups and out-groups persist in every society, even if they are not always visible to us. Pick any country today and you can find examples of marginalized people: In 2023 Seattle became the first city in the United States to ban discrimination based on caste, which is a way of dividing people based on their birth or descent that crosses ethnic, racial, and religious categories. The law was prompted by evidence of discrimination against members of the Dalit caste, a group that has suffered at the bottom of the social hierarchy in South Asia.[2] Although Denmark has been lauded for its progressive family policies that allow parents to manage work and caregiving responsibilities, its government policies from housing to head coverings have made non-White Muslim immigrants feel unwelcome.[3] Homosexuality is illegal in sixty-nine countries, primarily in Africa and the Caribbean, and punishable by death in eleven.[4] In 2023 Canada published a travel advisory warning to LGBTQ+ residents who wish to travel to the United States.[5] Inequality persists around the world despite the clear progress we have made over three-quarters of a century to establish universal human rights.

Many of us will be tested to welcome the continued stream of newcomers into our communities and workplaces because our instincts to distrust people who are different from us will kick in. Even if we consider ourselves educated and aware, we will always have to work toward understanding each other if we are to get along and be better citizens of the world. There is no way around it. Diversity is a fact. Inclusion is an act. When we commit to diversity, equity, and inclusion, we gain the power to make a difference. We can make our organizations, our communities, our nations, and the world more welcoming places where all can prosper. And no one will lose.

People First

With this book, I have given you a foundation to make your organization one of those places, and to sustain a culture that welcomes the full range of humanity. Sustainability entails integrating diversity, equity, and inclusion into how you operate daily. Your policies, processes, and management practices form the scaffolding for how you make decisions. Beyond these, you should have a people-first philosophy in all things, which means you may spend your time differently.

It only takes a few minutes to connect with a fellow human. All it takes is to ask each person one powerful question about themselves and their work, and focus on them, like the authority they are, when they answer. I like author Marcus Buckingham's suggestion for a weekly check-in: "What are your priorities this week, and how can I help?"[6] Or perhaps: "My goal is to help you succeed; what does that look like for you?" "What inspires you?" Or simply, "What would you like to talk about today?" You should have deeper conversations, too. But checking in with your people and following through with what they need shows them you see and care about them. Whatever time you spend with them, individually and as a team, it's not enough. Consider doubling it. Unless you create a workplace where everyone feels included and supported like this, you will not have the leaders you need in the future.

People first means you manage for them, not for a set of numbers. When you make decisions, you start with the stories of your employees, customers, suppliers, and partners before you delve into your financials. Remember what I said at the beginning: it is people who do the work, who make the customer experience sweet or sour, who make the profits or achieve the mission. Without people doing their best work together, your organization will struggle to accomplish anything. Forward-looking leaders know that their long-term success depends on embracing—and standing up for—our interconnected, multiethnic, multicultural, multigenerational future.

The ABCD framework provides a new way of thinking about diversity, equity, and inclusion in your business and an approach for making it central to how you run it. I've shown you how to:

A—Align diversity, equity, and inclusion with your business priorities. Knowing what your organization needs to accomplish enables you to target your efforts. Like Mercedes Abramo at Cartier, you may be confronting a shift in the demographics of your customers, or like Maria Boulden at DuPont, you may be transforming a slumping business. Your organization will thrive with a leadership team that fully understands the path ahead because it represents your customers, your workforce, and the talent pool in your community, country, or region.

B—Build partnerships with key stakeholders. To change anything, you need influence, support, and action from people who are invested in the outcome. People like Codie Sanchez, who provided her friend with the motivation and encouragement to hire women for his advertising agency, or the middle managers at Rockwell Collins who needed to hire and retain thousands more engineers. Strong relationships with stakeholders are essential to implementing new product development processes, hiring practices, and a culture of equity and inclusion for all.

C—Cultivate a culture of role models. Employees will do what they believe will make them successful, so it's up to leaders to model how they should act. Like the former Procter & Gamble CEO Robert McDonald and Heward-Mills CEO Dyann Heward-Mills, you start with the values of your organization. Like Michael Frank at Monsanto, you encourage your team members to be curious, explore their blind spots, and make it safe to have uncomfortable conversations. And like Michael Santa Maria at Baker McKenzie, you collaborate with your team members, providing help and support for them to do their best work and pursue their career goals.

D—Define objectives and outcomes with data. We need data to reveal our institutional blind spots, to understand the opportunities that an equitable, inclusive workplace and a more diverse leadership team offer our organizations, and to track our progress. Segmenting your people data beyond the standard categories of gender, race, and ethnicity is just a start. When you analyze it and your customer, financial, and operations data along with external data, you will have deeper insight into who is missing and what you have to gain by including them. You will also see where they are getting stuck in your organization and use these insights, as we did at Baker McKenzie, to find and remove the obstacles to their advancement.

I have offered you a way to look at how you do business while embedding diversity, equity, and inclusion into everything you already do. How you proceed depends on what is important to your organization—not something I can know as I sit at my desk. I have also outlined how to identify and remove the obstacles to talented and qualified leaders or potential leaders being noticed and chosen, how to redefine the leadership pipeline to include them, how to make people leaders at all levels responsible for creating more diverse teams, and how to empower them to act.

Listen and Act

These are not one-off or short-term measures like a new product introduction, a sales campaign, or building a new factory. Diversity, equity, and inclusion require constant attention for the reasons I've outlined. We are always encountering new people and situations where our instincts challenge our trust.

You will need a skilled, business-savvy diversity, equity, and inclusion leader who is a trusted advisor. This leader will guide you as your organization defines its goals; devises a strategy; creates the systems, policies, processes, and programs to execute it; and pursues change.

There is no silver bullet. Your organization's leaders and managers will need clarity, vision, and patience. They will need to commit to seeing changes through and adapting their approach as the workplace evolves. You wouldn't expect your organization to change its financial reporting processes overnight, either; they took years and many resources to build.

Above all, keep asking who is missing. Who is missing from the team, the pipeline, the meeting, the talent pool? Make this your mantra whenever you are making a decision that affects people (which is every decision). Bring the outsiders into your circle. Create teams that represent the world that we live in. And while you plan for tomorrow, stay curious.

What do I know?

What don't I know?

Who do I need to know?

Listen. Observe. Act. And watch your organization flourish.

Acknowledgments

It was my Baker McKenzie family who first heard the idea of my writing this book and who, without hesitation, and with great enthusiasm and vigor, threw their mightiest weight of support behind me. Before I thought of it, they offered and connected me to the many lawyers I interviewed for this book (not all of whom I quoted, but whose input shaped my thinking). They provided the wind beneath my wings that enabled me to take flight, and I owe them endlessly.

While working at Baker McKenzie, I met Laurie Cunningham. She is the sharpest and wittiest writer I have ever met, and I am privileged to have worked with her. She carefully laid every brick that served as the foundation for the book. Just like it was yesterday, I recall the conversation where she sweetly introduced the idea of me talking with her friend Bob Buday, a brilliant practitioner of thought leadership. While I had been published before, this was my first foray into conceiving a book idea and having serious plans to write it. Not knowing what that entailed, and inspired by how she described his expertise, I was instantly weak in the knees at the possibility of working with him.

Bob and his team patiently guided me through the entire process, including having me write articles where I could develop my thinking. Along the way, he gave me unfettered access to his vast bank of wisdom and flung open his Rolodex of contacts. I am grateful for all of it.

That is how I met Elana Varon. While I did not understand how listening to my presentations and our almost weekly Zoom calls would enable Elana to write in my voice, I trusted her and the process from the start. A wickedly patient, curious, and relentlessly hardworking being, she exceeded my expectations in all the ways possible. I lost count of the revisions to the proposal and the manuscript. She did them all. Without her expert guidance and kindness, this book would not have taken the shape it has. I could not and would not have birthed it without her. Elana, you've kept me sharp and open and helped me to embody my power. I appreciate you.

Elana introduced me to Madeleine McCullough, who was a college student when she signed on as my research assistant and stuck with this project beyond her graduation, to the end. Madeleine brought her sharp intellect and careful eye to every task, from assembling studies on more than a dozen topics to verifying my notes in the final manuscript. Madeleine, thank you.

There's a long list of people I interviewed and people who made introductions—too many to name. So to all of you, from Africa to Asia, Canada to China, Malaysia to Mexico, and the United Kingdom to the United States, thank you for your insights, hindsight, and foresight. Your kindness was borderless and boundless. Richard Morris, you showed confidence in my plan and gave me good advice about my first book proposal draft. That gave me the extra juice I needed in my battery to keep going. Thank you.

The universe opened up and conspired to give me all the ingredients I needed, including meeting Emily Taber by chance. Emily, you saw the value in my writing and encouraged me to pitch my proposal to the MIT Press. Catherine Woods, you, and your editorial team at the MIT Press, including Anne-Marie Bono, Virginia Crossman, Laura Keeler, and Emily Simon, guided me through the process. Your enthusiasm, creativity, and championing of authors show in everything you do. Thanks to all of you, this book is both different from and better than my original vision. I am so grateful to be in your orbit.

Augusto Alvarenga, your lively graphics helped me achieve my goal of a business book that puts people at the center by turning my lists and process diagrams into engaging figures. I appreciate your creativity.

Amy Appleyard, Wendy Jean Bennett, Emily Brower, Antoine Destin, Andy Eschtruth, Meg Gorecki, Chad Johnson, Stacy McKenna, and Elizabeth Moore: thank you for your close reading of the manuscript at various stages. You shared how you would use the book with your teams, what resonated with you, and what was missing. I appreciate your time, your spot-on suggestions, and your belief in the value of my work.

To my family in the United States and especially those in the United Kingdom who coached and cheered me on throughout this journey: you have been by my side with this book from the time of seed to the time of the harvest. To all my friends who walk with me under my umbrella, the Wolf Pack, and my colleagues and acquaintances, you never wavered in your enthusiasm, kindness, and care.

I am who I am, and I am where I am, because of all of you.

Notes

Introduction

1. Timothy Besley et al., "Gender Quotas and the Crisis of the Mediocre Man: Theory and Evidence from Sweden," *American Economic Review* 107, no. 8 (2017): 2204–2242, http://eprints.lse.ac.uk/69193/.

2. *2022 Edelman Trust Barometer* (Chicago: Edelman, 2022), https://www.edelman.com/trust/2022-trust-barometer.

3. "Household Data Annual Averages: Employed Persons by Detailed Occupation, Sex, Race, and Hispanic or Latino Ethnicity," Labor Force Statistics from the Current Population Survey, US Bureau of Labor Statistics, last modified January 25, 2023, https://www.bls.gov/cps/cpsaat11.htm.

4. Paige McGlauflin, "The Number of Black Fortune 500 CEOs Returns to Record High—Meet the 6 Chief Executives," *Fortune*, May 23, 2022, https://fortune.com/2022/05/23/meet-6-black-ceos-fortune-500-first-black-founder-to-ever-make-list/; Katharina Buchholz, "How Has the Number of Female CEOs in Fortune 500 Companies Changed over the Last 20 Years?," World Economic Forum, March 10, 2022, https://www.weforum.org/agenda/2022/03/ceos-fortune-500-companies-female.

Chapter 1

1. Anna Zakrzewski et al., "Managing the Next Decade of Women's Wealth," Boston Consulting Group, April 9, 2020, https://www.bcg.com/publications/2020/managing-next-decade-women-wealth; "Women: Primed and Ready for Progress," Nielsen, October 2019, https://www.nielsen.com/insights/2019/women-primed-and-ready-for-progress/.

2. Sylvia Anne Hewlett, Andrea Turner Moffitt, and Melinda Marshall, *Harnessing the Power of the Purse: Female Investors and Global Opportunities for Growth* (New York: Center for Talent Innovation, 2014), https://thegiin.org/research/publication/harnessing-the-power-of-the-purse-female-investors-and-global-opportunities-fo/.

3. *Diversity, Equity & Inclusion Benchmarking Survey: Global Data Sheet* (London: PwC, July 2022), https://www.pwc.com/gx/en/services/people-organisation/global-diversity-and-inclusion-survey/global-report-2022.pdf.

4. Frank Dobbins and Alexandra Kalev, *Getting to Diversity: What Works and What Doesn't* (Cambridge, MA: Belknap Press of Harvard University Press, 2023), 11.

5. Ruth Umoh, "A Recent Study Says Some White Men Feel Excluded at Work," CNBC, October 12, 2017, https://www.cnbc.com/2017/10/12/a-recent-study-says-some-white-men-feel-excluded-at-work.html.

6. Tessa L. Dover, Brenda Major, and Cheryl R. Kaiser, "Diversity Policies Rarely Make Companies Fairer, and They Feel Threatening to White Men," *Harvard Business Review*, January 4, 2016, https://hbr.org/2016/01/diversity-policies-dont-help-women-or-minorities-and-they-make-white-men-feel-threatened. The article describes the authors' research in the following paper: Tessa L. Dover, Brenda Major, and Cheryl R. Kaiser, "Members of High-Status Groups Are Threatened by Pro-Diversity Organizational Messages," *Journal of Experimental Social Psychology* 62 (2016): 58–67, https://doi.org/10.1016/j.jesp.2015.10.006.

7. Ernesto Dal Bó and Pedro Dal Bó, "'Do the Right Thing': The Effects of Moral Suasion on Cooperation," *Journal of Public Economics* 117 (2014): 28–38, https://doi.org/10.1016/j.jpubeco.2014.05.002.

8. *The Daily Show*, "Sallie Krawcheck—How Ellevest Is Challenging the Gender Investing Gap," interview by Trevor Noah, YouTube, February 5, 2019, https://www.youtube.com/watch?v=mdxS8S_06VM.

9. Anna Brown (Chief Inclusion and Diversity Officer, Baker McKenzie) in discussion with author via video, April 30, 2020.

10. *Diversity and Inclusion at Sodexo: Making a World of Difference*, Sodexo Quality of Life Services, 2018, https://tracks.sodexonet.com/files/live/sites/com-se/files/PDF/D&IAnnualReport.pdf.

11. Rohini Anand, "Learn with Your Peers: Strategies for Overcoming D E & I Challenges in the Boardroom," National Association of Corporate Directors, online panel discussion, July 11, 2023. Reported by the author.

12. Claudine Gartenberg, Andrea Madras Prat, and George Serafeim, "Corporate Purpose and Financial Performance," *Organization Science* 30, no. 1 (October 2018): 25, https://doi.org/10.1287/orsc.2018.1230.

13. Ethan McCarty, "The 'Great Resignation': The Perils of Misaligned Employee/Employer Values," Columbia University School of Professional Studies, November 4, 2021, https://sps.columbia.edu/news/great-resignation-perils-misaligned-employee employer-values.

14. For analysis of this phenomenon during mergers, see Margaret Cording et al., "Walking the Talk: A Multistakeholder Exploration of Organizational Authenticity, Employee Productivity, and Post-Merger Performance," *Academy of Management Perspectives* 28, no. 1 (October 2013): 38–56, https://doi.org/10.5465/amp.2013.0002.

15. "Business Roundtable Redefines the Purpose of a Corporation to Promote 'An Economy That Serves All Americans,'" Business Roundtable, August 19, 2019, https://www.businessroundtable.org/business-roundtable-redefines-the-purpose-of-a-corporation-to-promote-an-economy-that-serves-all-americans.

16. Stavros Gadinis and Amelia Miazad, "A Test of Stakeholder Capitalism," *Journal of Corporation Law* 47, no.1 (2022): 50–58.

17. Bruce Boyd (Principal, Arabella Advisors) in discussion with the author via video, January 16, 2023.

18. Robert McDonald (8th Secretary, US Department of Veterans Affairs, and retired Chairman, President, and Chief Executive Officer, Procter & Gamble), in discussion with the author via telephone, March 13, 2019.

19. Alana Wise, "Biden Pledged Historic Cabinet Diversity. Here's How His Nominees Stack Up," NPR, February 5, 2021, https://www.npr.org/sections/president-biden-takes-office/2021/02/05/963837953/biden-pledged-historic-cabinet-diversity-heres-how-his-nominees-stack-up.

20. Exec. Order No. 14035, 86 Fed. Reg. 34593 (June 30, 2021).

21. Jim O'Sullivan, "Remember Mitt Romney's 'Binders Full of Women?' They're Real. And We Got Them," *Boston Globe*, April 10, 2017, https://www.bostonglobe.com/metro/2017/04/10/romney-binders-still-full-women-are-unearthed/NTdYraj1yQ53uVklgnHZtL/story.html?event=event12.

Chapter 2

1. Dana M. Peterson and Catherine L. Mann, *Closing the Racial Inequality Gaps: The Economic Cost of Black Inequality in the U.S.* (New York: Citi Global Perspectives and Solutions, September 2020), 3, https://ir.citi.com/%2FPRxPvgNWu319AU1ajGf%2BsKbjJjBJSaTOSdw2DF4xynPwFB8a2jV1FaA3Idy7vY59bOtN2lxVQM%3D.

2. Nigel Springett, "Evaluating Corporate Purposes by the Psychological Contracts They Produce," *Strategic Change* 14, no. 7 (November 2005): 361–363, https://doi.org/10.1002/jsc.738.

3. Tracey Gray-Walker (CEO, AVMA Trust), in discussion with the author via video, December 28, 2022.

4. Jonathan Dunn et al., "Black Representation in Film and TV: The Challenges and Impact of Increasing Diversity," McKinsey, March 11, 2021, https://www.mckinsey

.com/featured-insights/diversity-and-inclusion/black-representation-in-film-and-tv
-the-challenges-and-impact-of-increasing-diversity.

5. Eva Rothenberg, "*Barbie* Makes History with $1 Billion at the Box Office," CNN, August 6, 2023, https://www.cnn.com/2023/08/06/business/barbie-box-office-history /index.html.

6. Rich Blake, "Fidelity Study Shows Economic Upside of Committing to Diversity," *Portfolio*, December 13, 2018, https://portfolio.bisanet.org/Article/fidelity-study-shows -economic-upside-of-committing-to-diversity.

7. "About Fidelity," Fidelity Investments, accessed February 24, 2023, https://www .fidelity.com/about-fidelity/our-company.

8. Peggy Collins and Charles Stein, "The Most Powerful Woman in Investing Gives a Rare Interview," *Bloomberg*, November 17, 2018, https://www.bloomberg.com /news/features/2018-11-17/fidelity-s-abby-johnson-opens-up-about-crypto-and -index-funds.

9. Mercedes Abramo (Deputy Chief Commercial Officer, Cartier International) in discussion with the author via telephone, December 17, 2020.

10. Brecken Branstrator, "Study: 51 Percent of Millennial Women Buy Jewelry for Themselves," *National Jeweler*, August 10, 2018, https://nationaljeweler.com/articles /2082-study-51-percent-of-millennial-women-buy-jewelry-for-themselves.

11. Abramo, discussion.

12. Ian Worthington et al., "Researching the Drivers of Socially Responsible Purchasing: A Cross-National Study of Supplier Diversity Initiatives," *Journal of Business Ethics* 79, no. 3 (May 2008): 327–328, https://doi.org/10.1007/s10551-007-9400-x.

13. John W. Rogers Jr., "Leaning into Business Diversity," interview by Chanda Smith Baker, August 27, 2021, in *Conversations with Chanda*, produced by Minneapolis Foundation, podcast, 42:00, https://www.minneapolisfoundation.org/podcasts /conversations-with-chanda/leaning-into-business-diversity/.

14. MarySue Barrett, "Equity in Action: How the University of Chicago Became a Trailblazer on Diversity in Professional Services," Metropolitan Planning Council, July 1, 2020, https://www.metroplanning.org/news/8906/Equity-in-Action-How-the -University-of-Chicago-Became-a-Trailblazer-on-Diversity-in-Professional-Services.

15. Roderick M. Kramer, "Rethinking Trust," *Harvard Business Review*, June 2009, https://hbr.org/2009/06/rethinking-trust.

16. Justine E. Tinkler et al., "Gender and Venture Capital Decision-Making: The Effects of Technical Background and Social Capital on Entrepreneurial Evaluations," *Social Science Research* 51 (2015): 1–16, https://doi.org/10.1016/j.ssresearch.2014.12 .008.

17. Sam Dewey, "Chicago's 4D Healthware Raised a $710K Seed Round. Here's Why It Matters," Built in Chicago, February 29, 2016, https://www.builtinchicago.org /2016/02/29/4dhealthware-star-cunningham-funding.

18. "Median Angel and Seed Deal Size Will Continute to Climb," *PitchBook Blog*, August 14, 2019, https://pitchbook.com/blog/median-angel-and-seed-deal-size-will -continue-to-climb.

19. "4D Healthware: Recent News and Activity," Crunchbase, October 12, 2021, https://www.crunchbase.com/organization/4d-healthware/company_overview/over view_timeline.

20. *The Equity Record, 2022 Edition* (London: Diversity VC, 2022), 11–14, https:// diversity.vc/diversity-vc-report-2022-usa/. Data from this report shows that Star Cunningham's experience remains typical. In 2022, more than a decade after she launched her company, 69 percent of decision-makers at venture funds were male, and 86 percent were White. They allocated less than 2 percent of their investments—$582 million out of $31.6 billion—to startups with only female or non-White founders.

21. Kate R. Lorig et al., "Evidence Suggesting that a Chronic Disease Self-Management Program Can Improve Health Status while Reducing Hospitalization," *Medical Care* 37, no. 1 (January 1999): 5–14, https://doi.org/10.1097/00005650-199901000-00003.

22. Latoya Hill, Nambi Ndugga, and Samantha Artiga, "Key Data on Health and Health Care by Race and Ethnicity," Kaiser Family Foundation, March 15, 2023, https://www.kff.org/racial-equity-and-health-policy/report/key-data-on-health-and -health-care-by-race-and-ethnicity/#HealthStatus.

23. Star Cunningham (Founder and CEO, 4D Healthware), in discussion with the author, May 17, 2018.

24. "An Interview with Esther Dyson," Ascent, September 10, 2020, https://web .archive.org/web/20230321150429/https://www.ascentconf.com/blog/an-interview -with-esther-dyson/.

25. Cunningham, discussion.

26. Rocio Lorenzo et al., "How Diverse Leadership Teams Boost Innovation," Boston Consulting Group, January 23, 2018, https://www.bcg.com/publications/2018/how -diverse-leadership-teams-boost-innovation.

27. McDonald, discussion.

28. Martin Reeves et al., "The Truth about Corporate Transformation," *MIT Sloan Management Review*, January 31, 2018, https://sloanreview.mit.edu/article/the-truth -about-corporate-transformation/.

29. Maria Boulden (Vice President, Executive Partner, Sales, Gartner), interview with Elana Varon, March 28, 2019.

30. Alan Góis et al., "Corporate Reputation and Bankruptcy Risk," *Brazilian Administration Review* 17, no. 2 (2020): 1–22, https://doi.org/10.1590/1807-7692bar2020 180159.

31. *2019 Edelman Trust Barometer Global Report* (Chicago: Edelman, 2019), https://www.edelman.com/sites/g/files/aatuss191/files/2019-02/2019_Edelman_Trust_Barom eter_Global_Report.pdf.

32. Daniel Cressey, "Monsanto Drops GM in Europe," *Nature* 499, no. 387 (2013), https://doi.org/10.1038/499387a.

33. Leticia Gonçalves (President, Global Foods, ADM), in discussion with the author, December 16, 2019.

34. Brad N. Greenwood, Seth Carnahan, and Laura Huang, "Patient & Physician Gender Concordance and Increased Mortality among Female Heart Attack Patients," *Proceedings of the National Academy of Sciences of the United States of America* 115, no. 34 (August 2018): 8569–8574, https://doi.org/10.1073/pnas.1800097115.

35. Katherine W. Phillips, Katie A. Liljenquist, and Margaret A. Neale, "Is the Pain Worth the Gain? The Advantages and Liabilities of Agreeing with Socially Distinct Newcomers," *Personality and Social Psychology Bulletin* 35, no. 3 (March 2009): 346–347, https://doi.org/10.1177/0146167208328062.

36. Christine Lagarde, "Women, Power and the Challenge of the Financial Crisis," *New York Times*, May 10, 2010, https://www.nytimes.com/2010/05/11/opinion/11iht -edlagarde.html?unlocked_article_code=1.aU0.8IgO.0sey9u0IHcTf&smid=url-share.

37. Poppy Harlow and Haley Draznin, "Bank of America's Anne Finucane: The 'Hippie' Turned Bank Exec," CNN Business, February 26, 2018, https://money.cnn .com/2018/02/26/news/companies/bank-of-america-anne-finucane/index.html.

38. Deborah Prenatt et al., "How Underdeveloped Decision Making and Poor Leadership Choices Led Kodak into Bankruptcy," *Journal of Modern Management & Entrepreneurship* 5, no. 1 (January 2015): 1–12.

Chapter 3

1. Codie A. Sanchez (Founder, Contrarian Thinking), in discussion with the author, July 19, 2018.

2. Mark M. Mendez (Partner, Davis Polk), in discussion with the author via telephone, October 11, 2018.

3. John Fialka, "Amazon Workers Win Climate Change Dispute, but It Is 'Not Enough,'" *Scientific American*, September 23, 2019, https://www.scientificamerican .com/article/amazon-workers-win-climate-dispute-but-it-is-not-enough/.

4. Jena McGregor, "Citigroup Is Revealing Pay Gap Data Most Companies Don't Want to Share," *Washington Post*, January 16, 2019, https://www.washingtonpost .com/business/2019/01/16/citigroup-is-revealing-pay-gap-data-most-companies-dont -want-share/.

5. Joseph Grenny et al., *Influencer: The New Science of Leading Change* (New York: McGraw Hill Education/VitalSmarts LLC, 2013), 71–73.

6. Abramo, discussion.

7. "In Focus: Shareholder Proposals in the 2023 U.S. Proxy Season," ISS Insights, July 20, 2023, https://insights.issgovernance.com/posts/in-focus-shareholder-proposal -in-the-2023-us-proxy-season/.

8. Richard Taylor (Senior Vice President of People Experience and Diversity, Nasdaq) in discussion with the author via video, January 5, 2023.

Chapter 4

1. Kate Sullivan (Host and Executive Producer, *To Dine For*) in discussion with the author, January 9, 2018.

2. Jami McKeon (Chair, Morgan Lewis) in discussion with the author via telephone, November 16, 2020.

3. David Gumbs (Principal, Global South, RMI) in discussion with the author via video, January 5, 2023.

4. Yannick Binvel et al., *The Global Talent Crunch* (Los Angeles: Korn Ferry, 2018), 4, https://www.kornferry.com/content/dam/kornferry/docs/pdfs/KF-Future-of-Work -Talent-Crunch-Report.pdf.

5. Jeff Schwartz et al., "The Worker-Employer Relationship Disrupted," *Deloitte Insights*, July 21, 2021, https://www2.deloitte.com/us/en/insights/focus/human-capital -trends/2021/the-evolving-employer-employee-relationship.html.

6. James Root et al., "Better with Age: The Rising Importance of Older Workers," Bain, 2023, https://www.bain.com/insights/better-with-age-the-rising-importance-of -older-workers/.

7. "Employment of Women on Nonfarm Payrolls by Industry Sector, Seasonally Adjusted," US Bureau of Labor Statistics, Table B-5, last modified February 3, 2023, https://www.bls.gov/news.release/empsit.t21.htm.

8. Katie Bell and Heidi Leeds, "Women in Healthcare: From the ER to the C-Suite," Korn Ferry, February 28, 2019, https://www.kornferry.com/insights/perspectives /perspective-women-in-healthcare.

9. Bryan Hancock et al., "Race in the Workplace: The Black Experience in the U.S. Private Sector," McKinsey, February 21, 2021, https://www.mckinsey.com/featured -insights/diversity-and-inclusion/race-in-the-workplace-the-black-experience-in-the -us-private-sector.

10. David F. Larker and Bryan Tayan, "Diversity in the C-Suite: The Dismal State of Diversity among Fortune 100 Senior Executives" (Rock Center for Corporate Governance at Stanford University Working Paper Series, Graduate School of Business, Stanford University, Stanford, CA, April 1, 2020), https://ssrn.com/abstract=3587498.

11. Peter Bailinson et al., "Understanding Organizational Barriers to a More Inclusive Workplace," McKinsey, June 23, 2020, https://www.mckinsey.com/capabilities /people-and-organizational-performance/our-insights/understanding-organizational -barriers-to-a-more-inclusive-workplace#/.

12. Ursula Burns, *Where You Are Is Not Who You Are: A Memoir* (New York: Amistad, 2021).

13. Natalie Alhonte Braga (Director of Strategy, Willkie Farr & Gallagher) in discussion with the author, October 16, 2018.

14. Madeleine Albright, presenter, National Association of Corporate Directors Global Board Leaders Summit, Chicago, October 4, 2017. Reported by the author.

15. Patrick M. Lencioni, "Make Your Values Mean Something," *Harvard Business Review*, July 2002, https://hbr.org/2002/07/make-your-values-mean-something.

16. Dyann Heward-Mills (CEO, Heward-Mills) in discussion with the author, May 4, 2018.

17. Helen Fagan and coauthors have identified seven attributes of inclusive leaders in an analysis of the research literature (authentic leadership, changemaker, collaborative, commitment to diversity and cultural competency, ideals, offers follower support, and openness), along with twenty-four impacts on followers' feelings of uniqueness and belonging. See Helen Abdali Soosan Fagan et al., "The Path to Inclusion: A Literature Review of the Attributes and Impacts of Inclusive Leaders," *Journal of Leadership Education* 29, no. 1 (January 2022): 95–101, https://doi.org/10.12806 /V21/I1/R7.

18. Nancy McGaw (Senior Advisor, Aspen Institute Business & Society Program), in discussion with the author, August 15, 2019.

19. "5 Whys," Lean Enterprise Institute, accessed February 12, 2024, https://www .lean.org/lexicon-terms/5-whys/.

20. Aileen Casanave (General Counsel, EarnUp) in discussion with the author, February 27, 2018.

21. Amy C. Edmondson, "Managing the Risk of Learning: Psychological Safety in Work Teams," in *International Handbook of Organizational Teamwork and Cooperative*

Working, ed. Michael A. West, Dean Tjosvold, and Ken G. Smith (Hoboken, NJ: Wiley, 2003), https://doi.org/10.1002/9780470696712.ch13.

22. "Census Bureau Releases New Data on Minority-Owned, Veteran-Owned and Women-Owned Businesses," US Census Bureau, November 10, 2022, https://www.census.gov/newsroom/press-releases/2022/annual-business-survey-characteristics.html.

23. "The Most Expensive Mistake Leaders Can Make," Gallup, accessed February 12, 2024, https://www.gallup.com/workplace/232964/expensive-mistake-leaders.aspx.

24. Michael Santa Maria (Partner, Baker McKenzie) in discussion with the author via telephone, July 16, 2018.

25. Hubert Joly, *The Heart of Business* (Cambridge, MA: Harvard Business Review Press, 2021), 184–185.

26. Lauren Landry, "What Is Human-Centered Design?," *Business Insights* (blog), updated January 6, 2023, https://online.hbs.edu/blog/post/what-is-human-centered-design#.

Chapter 5

1. Ranjay Gulati, "The Messy but Essential Pursuit of Business Purpose," *Harvard Business Review*, March–April 2022, https://hbr.org/2022/03/the-messy-but-essential-pursuit-of-purpose.

2. Milton L. Davenport III, DMD (Founder, Advanced Endodontics of Chicago), in discussion with the author, January 26, 2023.

3. Matt Downs (Managing Partner and Co-CEO, Sandbox Industries), in discussion with the author via telephone, August 21, 2018.

4. Spencer Rascoff, "Want to Further Gender Equality at Work? Do These 3 Things," *Inc.*, April 10, 2018, https://www.inc.com/spencer-rascoff/want-to-further-gender-equality-at-work-do-these-3-things.html.

5. Amy Feldman, "Doppler Labs Designed a Mini-Computer for Your Ears That It Hopes Will Make It the Next Apple," *Forbes*, October 19, 2016, https://www.forbes.com/sites/amyfeldman/2016/10/19/how-doppler-labs-designed-a-mini-computer-for-your-ears-it-hopes-will-be-the-next-big-thing/?sh=4dd99d1b2b3f.

6. K. R. Liu (Head of Brand Accessibility, Brand Studio, Google) in discussion with the author, July 30, 2018.

7. David Pierce, "Inside the Downfall of Doppler Labs," *Wired*, November 1, 2017, https://www.wired.com/story/inside-the-downfall-of-doppler-labs/.

8. Liu, discussion.

9. The White House, "Cheaper Hearing Aids Now in Stores Thanks to Biden-Harris Administration Competition Agenda," October 17, 2022, https://www.whitehouse .gov/briefing-room/statements-releases/2022/10/17/fact-sheet-cheaper-hearing-aids -now-in-stores-thanks-to-biden-harris-administration-competition-agenda/.

10. "Over-the-Counter Hearing Aids Market Size & Trends," Grand View Research, 2022, https://www.grandviewresearch.com/industry-analysis/over-the-counter-hearing -aids-market-report.

11. Umran Beba (retired Senior Vice President and Chief Global Diversity and Engagement Officer, PepsiCo), in discussion with the author via telephone, January 25, 2019.

12. "ESG Topics A-Z: Gender Parity," PepsiCo, June 28, 2023, https://www.pepsico .com/our-impact/esg-topics-a-z/gender-parity#.

13. Paula Santilli (CEO, Latin America, PepsiCo), interview with Elana Varon via telephone, January 8, 2020.

14. John H. Danley Jr. (Senior Director in the aerospace industry), in discussion with the author via video, January 18, 2023.

15. Santilli, interview.

16. Gray-Walker, discussion.

Chapter 6

1. US Bureau of Labor Statistics, "Household Data," Current Population Survey.

2. Dobbins and Kalev, *Getting to Diversity*, 128–129.

3. Gray-Walker, discussion.

4. Andres T. Tapia, Louis Montgomery, and Karen H. C. Huang, *The Next-Gen Chief Diversity Officer: An Evolving Profile of High-Impact D&I Executives* (Los Angeles: Korn Ferry, 2018), https://www.kornferry.com/content/dam/kornferry/docs/article-migra tion/NextGenerationCDO_Summer2018.pdf.

5. Denise Hamilton, "Don't Let Chief Diversity Officer Be a Dead-End Job," *Bloomberg*, January 18, 2021, https://www.bloomberg.com/opinion/articles/2021-01-18 /don-t-let-chief-diversity-officer-be-a-dead-end-job.

6. Tina Shah Paikeday et al., "A Global Look at the Chief Diversity Officer Landscape," Russell Reynolds Associates, April 21, 2023, https://www.russellreynolds.com /en/insights/reports-surveys/a-global-look-at-the-chief-diversity-officer-landscape.

7. Taylor, discussion.

8. Taylor, discussion.

9. Marcus Buckingham and Ashley Goodall, *Nine Lies about Work: A Freethinking Leader's Guide to the Real World* (Cambridge, MA: Harvard Business School Press, 2019), 32–33.

10. Stephanie Vaccari (Leader, Intellectual Property Tech Practice Group, Toronto, Baker McKenzie), in discussion with the author, August 4, 2020.

11. Michelle Peluso, Carolyn Heller Baird, and Lynn Kesterson-Townes, *Women, Leadership, and the Priority Paradox* (IBM Institute for Business Value, 2019), https://www.ibm.com/thought-leadership/institute-business-value/report/womeninleadership#.

12. Taylor, discussion.

13. Taylor, discussion.

14. Gonçalves, discussion.

15. Julie J. Eaton (Divisional CEO, Halma), in discussion with the author via telephone, April 30, 2019.

16. Taylor, discussion.

17. "Language Bias in Performance Feedback 2023," Textio, 2023, https://explore.textio.com/feedback-bias-2023.

18. Alice Eagly and Linda L. Carli, "Women and the Labyrinth of Leadership," *Harvard Business Review*, September 2007, https://hbr.org/2007/09/women-and-the-labyrinth-of-leadership; Daphna Motro et al., "The 'Angry Black Woman' Stereotype at Work," *Harvard Business Review*, January 31, 2022, https://hbr.org/2022/01/the-angry-black-woman-stereotype-at-work.

19. Erika V. Hall and Robert W. Livingston, "The Hubris Penalty: Biased Responses to 'Celebration' Displays of Black Football Players," *Journal of Experimental Social Psychology* 48, no. 4 (2012): 901, https://doi.org/10.1016/j.jesp.2012.02.004; John Paul Wilson, Kurt Hugenberg, and Nicholas O. Rule, "Racial Bias in Judgements of Physical Size and Formidability: From Size to Threat," *Journal of Personality and Social Psychology* 113, no. 1 (2017): 66, http://dx.doi.org/10.1037/pspi0000092.

20. Davenport, discussion.

21. McKeon, discussion.

22. Cecilia Kang, "Google Data-Mines Its Approach to Promoting Women," *Washington Post*, April 2, 2014, https://www.washingtonpost.com/news/the-switch/wp/2014/04/02/google-data-mines-its-women-problem/?noredirect=on.

Chapter 7

1. Mazen Fayad, Bobby Dhillon, and Nicolai Van Dirchsen, "Coca Cola—Labels Are for Cans, Not for People" (Pause Films, 2017), 2:48, https://vimeo.com/224673737.

2. Joan D. Chittister, *Scarred by Struggle, Transformed by Hope* (Grand Rapids, MI: Eerdmans, 2003), 69.

3. Boyd, discussion.

4. *Costly Conversations: Why Employee Communication Wrecks Your Bottom Line*, Crucial Learning, n.d., https://vitalsmarts.widen.net/s/mwwmcfmqbg/ebook---costly -conversations.

5. Davenport, discussion.

6. Santa Maria, discussion.

7. Danley, discussion.

8. Stephen M. R. Covey with Rebecca R. Merrill, *The Speed of Trust: The One Thing That Changes Everything* (New York: Free Press, 2006), 136–221.

9. Boulden, discussion.

10. Workforce Institute at UKG, *The Heard and the Heard-Nots* (Austin, TX: UKG, 2021), 10–11, https://workforceinstitute.org/wp-content/uploads/The-Heard-and-the -Heard-Nots.pdf.

11. Todd Rogers and Jessica Lasky-Fink, "Harvard Researchers Explain How Our Brains Skim Information and How to Actually Get People's Attention," *Fast Company*, September 12, 2023, https://www.fastcompany.com/90951313/harvard -researchers-explain-how-our-brains-skim-information-and-how-to-actually-get-peoples -attention.

Chapter 8

1. Sophie Heading and Saadi Zahidi, *Global Risks Report 2023*, World Economic Forum, January 11, 2023, 9, https://www.weforum.org/reports/global-risks-report -2023/.

2. Niha Masih, "Seattle Becomes the First U.S. City to Ban Caste Discrimination," *Washington Post*, February 22, 2023, https://www.washingtonpost.com/nation/2023 /02/21/seattle-caste-discrimination-ban/.

3. Somdeep Sen, "As Denmark Votes, I Have a Question: Am I Welcome Here?," *Al Jazeera*, November 1, 2022, https://www.aljazeera.com/opinions/2022/11/1/denmark -election-migrant-welcome.

4. Daniele Paletta, "ILGA World Updates State-Sponsored Homophobia Report: 'There's Progress in Times of Uncertainty,'" ILGA World, December 15, 2020, https://ilga.org/ilga-world-releases-state-sponsored-homophobia-December-2020-update.

5. Kiara Alfonseca, "Canada Issues Warning for LGBTQ Travelers in the United States," ABC News, August 30, 2023, https://abcnews.go.com/International/canada-issues-warning-lgbtq-travelers-united-states/story?id=102674189.

6. Marcus Buckingham TV, "The Check-In Conversation," YouTube, February 20, 2018, https://www.youtube.com/watch?v=MjYSlfGdNVk.

Bibliography

"4D Healthware: Recent News & Activity." Crunchbase, October 12, 2021. https://www.crunchbase.com/organization/4d-healthware/company_financials.

2012 Annual Report. Cincinnati: Proctor & Gamble, 2012. https://s1.q4cdn.com/695946674/files/doc_financials/2012/030bd639-dafa-2646-93c6-6ecd61f74e2f.pdf.

2019 Edelman Trust Barometer. Chicago: Edelman, 2019. https://www.edelman.com/sites/g/files/aatuss191/files/2019-02/2019_Edelman_Trust_Barometer_Global_Report.pdf.

2022 Edelman Trust Barometer. Chicago: Edelman, 2022. https://www.edelman.com/trust/2022-trust-barometer.

Alfonseca, Kiara. "Canada Issues Warning for LGBTQ Travelers in the United States." ABC News, August 30, 2023. https://abcnews.go.com/International/canada-issues-warning-lgbtq-travelers-united-states/story?id=102674189.

Bailinson, Peter, William Decherd, Diana Ellsworth, and Maital Guttman. "Understanding Organizational Barriers to a More Inclusive Workplace." McKinsey, June 23, 2020. https://www.mckinsey.com/capabilities/people-and-organizational-performance/our-insights/understanding-organizational-barriers-to-a-more-inclusive-workplace#/.

Barrett, MarySue. "Equity in Action: How the University of Chicago Became a Trailblazer on Diversity in Professional Services." Metropolitan Planning Council, July 1, 2020. https://www.metroplanning.org/news/8906/Equity-in-Action-How-the-University-of-Chicago-Became-a-Trailblazer-on-Diversity-in-Professional-Services.

Bell, Katie, and Heidi Leeds. "Women in Healthcare: From the ER to the C-Suite." Korn Ferry, February 28, 2019. https://www.kornferry.com/insights/perspectives/perspective-women-in-healthcare.

Besley, Timothy, Olle Folke, Torsten Persson, and Johanna Rickne. "Gender Quotas and the Crisis of the Mediocre Man: Theory and Evidence from Sweden." *American Economic Review* 107, no. 8 (2017): 2204–2242. http://eprints.lse.ac.uk/69193/.

Binvel, Yannick, Michael Franzino, Jean-Marc Laouchez, and Werner Penk. *The Global Talent Crunch*. Los Angeles: Korn Ferry, 2018. https://www.kornferry.com /content/dam/kornferry/docs/pdfs/KF-Future-of-Work-Talent-Crunch-Report.pdf.

Blake, Rich. "Fidelity Study Shows Economic Upside of Committing to Diversity." *Portfolio*, December 13, 2018. https://portfolio.bisanet.org/Article/fidelity-study-shows -economic-upside-of-committing-to-diversity.

Branstrator, Brecken. "Study: 51 Percent of Millennial Women Buy Jewelry for Themselves." *National Jeweler*, August 10, 2018. https://nationaljeweler.com/articles /2082-study-51-percent-of-millennial-women-buy-jewelry-for-themselves.

Brown, Karen. "To Retain Employees, Focus on Inclusion—Not Just Diversity." *Harvard Business Review*, December 4, 2018. https://hbr.org/2018/12/to-retain-employees -focus-on-inclusion-not-just-diversity.

Buchholz, Katharina. "How Has the Number of Female CEOs in Fortune 500 Companies Changed Over the Last 20 Years?" World Economic Forum, March 10, 2022. https://www.weforum.org/agenda/2022/03/ceos-fortune-500-companies-female.

Buckingham, Marcus, and Ashley Goodall. *Nine Lies about Work: A Freethinking Leader's Guide to the Real World*. Cambridge, MA: Harvard Business School Press, 2019.

Burns, Ursula. *Where You Are Is Not Who You Are: A Memoir*. New York: Amistad, 2021.

"Business Roundtable Redefines the Purpose of a Corporation to Promote 'An Economy That Serves All Americans.'" Business Roundtable, August 19, 2019. https:// www.businessroundtable.org/business-roundtable-redefines-the-purpose-of-a-corpo ration-to-promote-an-economy-that-serves-all-americans.

"Census Bureau Releases New Data on Minority-Owned, Veteran-Owned and Women-Owned Businesses." US Census Bureau, November 10, 2022. https://www.census .gov/newsroom/press-releases/2022/annual-business-survey-characteristics.html.

Chittister, Joan D. *Scarred by Struggle, Transformed by Hope*. Grand Rapids, MI: Eerdmans, 2003.

Collins, Peggy, and Charles Stein. "The Most Powerful Woman in Investing Gives a Rare Interview." *Bloomberg*, November 17, 2018. https://www.bloomberg.com/news /features/2018-11-17/fidelity-s-abby-johnson-opens-up-about-crypto-and-index-funds.

Cording, Margaret, Jeffrey S. Harrison, Robert E. Hoskisson, and Karsten Jonsen. "Walking the Talk: A Multistakeholder Exploration of Organizational Authenticity, Employee Productivity, and Post-Merger Performance." *Academy of Management Perspectives* 28, no. 1 (October 2013): 38–56. https://doi.org/10.5465/amp.2013.0002.

Costly Conversations: Why Employee Communication Wrecks Your Bottom Line. Crucial Learning. n.d. https://vitalsmarts.widen.net/s/mwwmcfmqbg/ebook---costly -conversations.

Covey, Stephen M. R., with Rebecca R. Merrill. *The Speed of Trust: The One Thing That Changes Everything*. New York: Free Press, 2006.

Creary, Stephanie J., Nancy Rothbard, and Jared Scruggs. *Evidence-Based Diversity, Equity, and Inclusion Practices*. Philadelphia: The Wharton School of the University of Pennsylvania, May 2021. https://www.wharton.upenn.edu/wp-content/uploads/2021/05/Applied-Insights-Lab-Report.pdf.

Cressey, Daniel. "Monsanto Drops GM in Europe." *Nature* 499, no. 387 (2013). https://doi.org/10.1038/499387a.

The Daily Show. "Sallie Krawcheck—How Ellevest Is Challenging the Gender Investing Gap." Interview by Trevor Noah. YouTube, February 5, 2019. https://www.youtube.com/watch?v=mdxS8S_06VM.

Dal Bó, Ernesto, and Pedro Dal Bó. "'Do the Right Thing': The Effects of Moral Suasion on Cooperation." *Journal of Public Economics* 117 (2014): 28–38. https://doi.org/10.1016/j.jpubeco.2014.05.002.

Dewey, Sam. "Chicago's 4D Healthware Raised a $710K Seed Round. Here's Why It Matters." Built In Chicago, February 29, 2016. https://www.builtinchicago.org/2016/02/29/4dhealthware-star-cunningham-funding.

Diversity and Inclusion at Sodexo: Making a World of Difference. Sodexo Quality of Life Services, 2018. https://tracks.sodexonet.com/files/live/sites/com-se/files/PDF/D&I AnnualReport.pdf.

Diversity, Equity & Inclusion Benchmarking Survey: Global Data Sheet. London: PwC, July 2022. https://www.pwc.com/gx/en/services/people-organisation/global-diversity-and-inclusion-survey/global-report-2022.pdf.

Dobbins, Frank, and Alexandra Kalev. *Getting to Diversity: What Works and What Doesn't*. Cambridge, MA: Belknap Press of Harvard University Press, 2022.

Dover, Tessa L., Brenda Major, and Cheryl R. Kaiser. "Diversity Policies Rarely Make Companies Fairer, and They Feel Threatening to White Men." *Harvard Business Review*, January 4, 2016. https://hbr.org/2016/01/diversity-policies-dont-help-women-or-minorities-and-they-make-white-men-feel-threatened.

Dunn, Jonathan, Sheldon Lyn, Nony Onyeador, and Ammanuel Zegeye. "Black Representation in Film and TV: The Challenges and Impact of Increasing Diversity." McKinsey, March 11, 2021. https://www.mckinsey.com/featured-insights/diversity-and-inclusion/black-representation-in-film-and-tv-the-challenges-and-impact-of-increasing-diversity.

Eagly, Alice, and Linda L. Carli. "Women and the Labyrinth of Leadership." *Harvard Business Review*, September 2007. https://hbr.org/2007/09/women-and-the-labyrinth-of-leadership.

Edmondson, Amy C. "Managing the Risk of Learning: Psychological Safety in Work Teams." In *International Handbook of Organizational Teamwork and Cooperative Working*, edited by Michael A. West, Dean Tjosvold, and Ken G. Smith. Hoboken, NJ: Wiley, 2003. https://doi.org/10.1002/9780470696712.ch13.

"Employment of Women on Nonfarm Payrolls by Industry Sector, Seasonally Adjusted." US Bureau of Labor Statistics, last modified February 3, 2023. https://www.bls.gov/news.release/empsit.t21.htm.

Epley, Nicholas. *Mindset: How We Understand What Others Think, Feel, Believe, and Want*. New York: Knopf, 2014.

"ESG Topics A-Z: Gender Parity." PepsiCo, updated June 28, 2023. https://www.pepsico.com/our-impact/esg-topics-a-z/gender-parity#.

Fagan, Helen Abdali Soosan, Samantha Guenther, Brooke Wells, and Gina S. Matkin. "The Path to Inclusion: A Literature Review of the Attributes and Impacts of Inclusive Leaders." *Journal of Leadership Education* 21, no. 1 (January 2022): 95–101. https://doi.org/10.12806/V21/I1/R7.

Fayad, Mazen, Bobby Dhillon, and Nicolai Van Dirchsen. "Coca Cola—Labels Are for Cans, Not for People." Pause Films, 2017. Vimeo video, 2:48. https://vimeo.com/224673737.

Feldman, Amy. "Doppler Labs Designed a Mini-Computer for Your Ears That It Hopes Will Make It the Next Apple." *Forbes*, October 19, 2016. https://www.forbes.com/sites/amyfeldman/2016/10/19/how-doppler-labs-designed-a-mini-computer-for-your-ears-it-hopes-will-be-the-next-big-thing/?sh=284aa3592b3f.

Fialka, John. "Amazon Workers Win Climate Change Dispute, but It Is 'Not Enough.'" *Scientific American*, September 23, 2019. https://www.scientificamerican.com/article/amazon-workers-win-climate-dispute-but-it-is-not-enough/.

Frei, Frances X., and Francesca Gino. "A World of Difference." Interview by Jen McFarland Flint. Alumni Bulletin, Harvard Business School, February 22, 2022. https://www.alumni.hbs.edu/stories/Pages/story-bulletin.aspx?num=8627.

Gartenberg, Claudine, Andrea Prat, and George Serafeim. "Corporate Purpose and Financial Performance." *Organization Science* 30, no. 1 (2019): 1–18. https://doi.org/10.1287/orsc.2018.1230.

Gadinis, Stavros, and Amelia Miazad. "A Test of Stakeholder Capitalism." *Journal of Corporation Law* 47, no. 1 (2022): 47–104.

Góis, Alan, Márcia De Luca, Gerlando de Lima, and Jislene Medeiros. "Corporate Reputation and Bankruptcy Risk." *Brazilian Administration Review* 17, no. 2 (2020): 1–22. https://doi.org/10.1590/1807-7692bar2020180159.

Greenwood, Brad N., Seth Carnahan, and Laura Huang. "Patient & Physician Gender Concordance and Increased Mortality among Female Heart Attack Patients." *Proceedings of the National Academy of Sciences of the United States of America* 115, no. 34 (2018): 8569–8574. https://doi.org/10.1073/pnas.1800097115.

Grenny, Joseph, Kerry Patterson, David Maxfield, Ron McMillan, and Al Switzler. *Influencer: The New Science of Leading Change.* New York: McGraw Hill Education/ VitalSmarts, 2013.

Gulati, Ranjay. "The Messy but Essential Pursuit of Business Purpose." *Harvard Business Review*, March–April 2022. https://hbr.org/2022/03/the-messy-but-essential -pursuit-of-purpose.

Hall, Erika V., and Robert Livingston. "The Hubris Penalty: Biased Responses to 'Celebration' Displays of Black Football Players." *Journal of Experimental Social Psychology* 48, no. 4 (July 2012): 899–904. https://doi.org/10.1016/j.jesp.2012.02.004.

Hamilton, Denise. "Don't Let Chief Diversity Officer Be a Dead-End Job." *Bloomberg*, January 18, 2021. https://www.bloomberg.com/opinion/articles/2021-01-18/don't -let-chief-diversity-officer-be-a-dead-end-job.

Hancock, Bryan, Monne Williams, James Manyika, Lareina Yee, and Jackie Wong. "Race in the Workplace: The Black Experience in the U.S. Private Sector." McKinsey, February 21, 2021. https://www.mckinsey.com/featured-insights/diversity-and -inclusion/race-in-the-workplace-the-black-experience-in-the-us-private-sector.

Harlow, Poppy, and Haley Draznin. "Bank of America's Anne Finucane: The 'Hippie' Turned Bank Exec." CNN Business, February 26, 2018. https://money.cnn.com/2018 /02/26/news/companies/bank-of-america-anne-finucane/index.html.

Heading, Sophie, and Saadi Zahidi. *Global Risks Report 2023.* World Economic Forum, January 11, 2023. https://www.weforum.org/reports/global-risks-report-2023/.

"HeForShe Data Trends." UN Women, 2021. https://www.heforshe.org/sites/default /files/2021-07/hfs2021_data_trends.pdf.

Hewlett, Sylvia Anne, Andrea Turner Moffitt, and Melinda Marshall. *Harnessing the Power of the Purse: Female Investors and Opportunities for Global Growth.* New York: Center for Talent Innovation, 2014. https://thegiin.org/research/publication/har nessing-the-power-of-the-purse-female-investors-and-global-opportunities-fo/.

Hill, Latoya, Nambi Ndugga, and Samantha Artiga. "Key Data on Health and Health Care by Race and Ethnicity." Kaiser Family Foundation, March 15, 2023. https:// www.kff.org/racial-equity-and-health-policy/report/key-data-on-health-and-health -care-by-race-and-ethnicity/#HealthStatus.

"In Focus: Shareholder Proposals in the 2023 U.S. Proxy Season." ISS Insights, July 20, 2023. https://insights.issgovernance.com/posts/in-focus-shareholder-proposal-in -the-2023-us-proxy-season/.

"An Interview with Esther Dyson." Ascent, September 10, 2020. https://web.archive .org/web/20230321150429/https://www.ascentconf.com/blog/an-interview-with -esther-dyson/.

Investment Stewardship 2018 Annual Report. New York: BlackRock, 2018. https://www .blackrock.com/corporate/literature/publication/blk-annual-stewardship-report -2018.pdf.

Investment Stewardship Annual Report, January 1–December 31, 2021. New York: Black-Rock, 2021. https://www.blackrock.com/corporate/literature/publication/annual-stew ardship-report-2021.pdf.

Joly, Hubert. *The Heart of Business.* Cambridge, MA: Harvard Business Review Press, 2021.

Kang, Cecilia. "Google Data-Mines Its Approach to Promoting Women." *Washington Post,* April 2, 2014. https://www.washingtonpost.com/news/the-switch/wp/2014/04 /02/google-data-mines-its-women-problem/?noredirect=on.

Kramer, Roderick M. "Rethinking Trust." *Harvard Business Review,* June 2009. https:// hbr.org/2009/06/rethinking-trust.

Lagarde, Christine. "Women, Power, and the Challenge of the Financial Crisis." *New York Times,* May 10, 2010. https://www.nytimes.com/2010/05/11/opinion/11iht -edlagarde.html?unlocked_article_code=1.aU0.8IgO.0sey9u0IHcTf&smid=url-share.

Landry, Lauren. "What Is Human-Centered Design?" *Business Insights* (blog), updated January 6, 2023. https://online.hbs.edu/blog/post/what-is-human-centered-design#.

"Language Bias in Performance Feedback 2023." Textio, 2023. https://explore.textio .com/feedback-bias-2023.

Larker, David F., and Bryan Tayan. "Diversity in the C-Suite: The Dismal State of Diversity among Fortune 100 Senior Executives." Rock Center for Corporate Governance at Stanford University Working Paper Series, Graduate School of Business, Stanford University, Stanford, CA, April 1, 2020. https://ssrn.com/abstract=3587498.

Lencioni, Patrick M. "Make Your Values Mean Something." *Harvard Business Review,* July 2002, https://hbr.org/2002/07/make-your-values-mean-something.

Lorenzo, Rocio, Nicole Voigt, Miki Tsusaka, and Matt Krentz. "How Diverse Leadership Teams Boost Innovation." Boston Consulting Group, 2018. https://www.bcg .com/publications/2018/how-diverse-leadership-teams-boost-innovation.

Lorig, Kate R., David S. Sobel, Anita L. Stewart, Byron William Brown Jr., Albert Bandura, Philip Ritter, Virginia M. Gonzalez, Diana D. Laurent, and Halsted R. Holman. "Evidence Suggesting that a Chronic Disease Self-Management Program Can Improve Health Status while Reducing Hospitalization." *Medical Care* 37, no.1 (January 1999): 5–14. https://doi.org/10.1097/00005650-199901000-00003.

Marcus Buckingham TV. "The Check-In Conversation." YouTube, February 20, 2018. https://www.youtube.com/watch?v=MjYSlfGdNVk.

Masih, Niha. "Seattle Becomes the First U.S. City to Ban Caste Discrimination." *Washington Post*, February 22, 2023. https://www.washingtonpost.com/nation/2023/02/21 /seattle-caste-discrimination-ban/.

McCarty, Ethan. "The 'Great Resignation': The Perils of Misaligned Employee/ Employer Values." Columbia University School of Professional Studies, November 4, 2021. https://sps.columbia.edu/news/great-resignation-perils-misaligned-employee employer-values.

McGlauflin, Paige. "The Number of Black Fortune 500 CEOs Returns to Record High— Meet the 6 Chief Executives." *Fortune*, May 23, 2022. https://fortune.com/2022/05/23 /meet-6-black-ceos-fortune-500-first-black-founder-to-ever-make-list/.

McGregor, Jena. "Citigroup Is Revealing Pay Gap Data Most Companies Don't Want to Share." *Washington Post*, January 16, 2019. https://www.washingtonpost.com /business/2019/01/16/citigroup-is-revealing-pay-gap-data-most-companies-dont -want-share/.

"Median Angel and Seed Deal Size Will Continue to Climb." *PitchBook Blog*, August 14, 2019. https://pitchbook.com/blog/median-angel-and-seed-deal-size-will-continue -to-climb.

"The Most Expensive Mistake Leaders Can Make." Gallup. Accessed February 12, 2024. https://www.gallup.com/workplace/232964/expensive-mistake-leaders.aspx.

Motro, Daphna, Jonathan B. Evans, Aleksander P. J. Ellis, and Lehman Benson III. "The 'Angry Black Woman' Stereotype at Work." *Harvard Business Review*, January 31, 2022. https://hbr.org/2022/01/the-angry-black-woman-stereotype-at-work.

Netchaeva, Ekaterina. "Women Are Still Less Likely to Aspire to Leadership in Business, Despite Decades of Gender Initiatives—We Need to Find Out Why." *The Conversation*, June 29, 2022. https://theconversation.com/women-are-still-less-likely-to -aspire-to-leadership-in-business-despite-decades-of-gender-initiatives-we-need-to -find-out-why-185796.

O'Sullivan, Jim. "Remember Mitt Romney's 'Binders Full of Women?' They're Real. And We Got Them." *Boston Globe*, April 10, 2017. https://www.bostonglobe.com /metro/2017/04/10/romney-binders-still-full-women-are-unearthed/NTdYraj1yQ53 uVklgnHZtL/story.html?event=event12.

Paikeday, Tina Shah, Nisa Qosja, Shoon Lim, and Jennifer Flock. "A Global Look at the Chief Diversity Officer Landscape." Russell Reynolds Associates, April 21, 2023. https://www.russellreynolds.com/en/insights/reports-surveys/a-global-look-at-the -chief-diversity-officer-landscape.

Paletta, Daniele. "ILGA World Updates State-Sponsored Homophobia Report: 'There's Progress in Times of Uncertainty.'" ILGA World, December 15, 2020. https://ilga.org/ilga-world-releases-state-sponsored-homophobia-December-2020-update.

Peluso, Michelle, Carolyn Heller Baird, and Lynn Kesterson-Townes. *Women, Leadership, and the Priority Paradox.* IBM Institute for Business Value, 2019. https://www.ibm.com/thought-leadership/institute-business-value/report/womeninleadership#.

Peterson, Dana M., and Catherine Mann. *Closing the Racial Inequality Gaps: The Economic Cost of Black Inequality in the U.S.* New York: Citi Global Perspectives and Solutions, September 2020. https://ir.citi.com/%2FPRxPvgNWu319AU1ajGf%2BsKbjJjBJSaTOSdw2DF4xynPwFB8a2jV1FaA3Idy7vY59bOtN2lxVQM%3D.

Phillips, Katherine W., Katie A. Liljenquist, and Margaret A. Neale. "Is the Pain Worth the Gain? The Advantages and Liabilities of Agreeing with Socially Distinct Newcomers." *Personality and Social Psychology Bulletin* 35, no. 3 (March 2009): 336–350. https://doi.org/10.1177/0146167208328062.

Pierce, David. "Inside the Downfall of Doppler Labs." *Wired*, November 1, 2017. https://www.wired.com/story/inside-the-downfall-of-doppler-labs/.

Prenatt, Deborah, James Ondracek, M. Saeed, and Andy Bertsch. "How Underdeveloped Decision Making and Poor Leadership Choices Led Kodak into Bankruptcy." *Journal of Modern Management & Entrepreneurship* 5, no. 1 (January 2015): 1–12.

Rascoff, Spencer. "Want to Further Gender Equality at Work? Do These 3 Things." *Inc.*, April 10, 2018. https://www.inc.com/spencer-rascoff/want-to-further-gender-equality-at-work-do-these-3-things.html.

Reeves, Martin, Lars Fæste, Kevin Whitaker, and Fabien Hassan. "The Truth about Corporate Transformation." *MIT Sloan Management Review*, January 31, 2018. https://sloanreview.mit.edu/article/the-truth-about-corporate-transformation/.

Rogers, John W., Jr. "Leaning into Business Diversity." Interview by Chanda Smith Baker, August 27, 2021. In *Conversations with Chanda*, produced by Minneapolis Foundation. Podcast, 42:00. https://www.minneapolisfoundation.org/podcasts/conversations-with-chanda/leaning-into-business-diversity/.

Rogers, Todd, and Jessica Lasky-Fink. "Harvard Researchers Explain How Our Brains Skim Information and How to Actually Get People's Attention." *Fast Company*, September 12, 2023. https://www.fastcompany.com/90951313/harvard-researchers-explain-how-our-brains-skim-information-and-how-to-actually-get-peoples-attention.

Root, James, Andrew Schwedel, Mike Haslett, and Nicole Bitler. "Better with Age: The Rising Importance of Older Workers." Bain, 2023. https://www.bain.com/insights/better-with-age-the-rising-importance-of-older-workers/.

Rothenberg, Eva. "*Barbie* Makes History with $1 Billion at the Box Office." CNN, August 6, 2023. https://www.cnn.com/2023/08/06/business/barbie-box-office-history /index.html.

Schwartz, Jeff, Kraig Eaton, David Mallon, Yves Van Durme, Maren Hauptmann, Shannon Poynton, and Nic Scoble-Williams. "The Worker-Employer Relationship Disrupted." *Deloitte Insights*, July 21, 2021. https://www2.deloitte.com/us/en /insights/focus/human-capital-trends/2021/the-evolving-employer-employee-rela tionship.html.

Sen, Somdeep. "As Denmark Votes, I Have a Question: Am I Welcome Here?" *Al Jazeera*, November 1, 2022. https://www.aljazeera.com/opinions/2022/11/1/denmark -election-migrant-welcome.

Springett, Nigel. "Evaluating Corporate Purposes by the Psychological Contracts They Produce." *Strategic Change* 14, no. 7 (November 2005): 357–366. https://doi.org /10.1002/jsc.738.

Tapia, Andres T., Louis Montgomery, and Karen H. C. Huang. *The Next-Gen Chief Diversity Officer: An Evolving Profile of High-Impact D&I Executives*. Los Angeles: Korn Ferry, 2018. https://www.kornferry.com/content/dam/kornferry/docs/article-migra tion/NextGenerationCDO_Summer2018.pdf.

Tinkler, Justine E., Kjersten Bunker Whittington, Manwai C. Ku, and Andrea Rees Davies. "Gender and Venture Capital Decision-Making: The Effects of Technical Background and Social Capital on Entrepreneurial Evaluations." *Social Science Research* 51 (2015): 1–16.

Umoh, Ruth. "A Recent Study Says Some White Men Feel Excluded at Work." CNBC, October 12, 2017. https://www.cnbc.com/2017/10/12/a-recent-study-says-some-white -men-feel-excluded-at-work.html.

"Vital Signs: African American Health." Centers for Disease Control and Prevention, updated July 3, 2017. https://archive.cdc.gov/www_cdc_gov/vitalsigns/aahealth /index.html.

Wilson, John Paul, Kurt Hugenberg, and Nicholas O. Rule. "Racial Bias in Judgements of Physical Size and Formidability: From Size to Threat." *Journal of Personality and Social Psychology* 113, no. 1 (2017): 59–80. http://dx.doi.org/10.1037/pspi0000092.

Wise, Alana. "Biden Pledged Historic Cabinet Diversity. Here's How His Nominees Stack Up." NPR, February 5, 2021. https://www.npr.org/sections/president-biden -takes-office/2021/02/05/963837953/biden-pledged-historic-cabinet-diversity-heres -how-his-nominees-stack-up.

"Women: Primed and Ready for Progress." Nielsen, October 2019. https://www .nielsen.com/insights/2019/women-primed-and-ready-for-progress/.

Workforce Institute at UKG. *The Heard and the Heard-Nots.* Austin, TX: UKG, 2021. https://workforceinstitute.org/wp-content/uploads/The-Heard-and-the-Heard-Nots .pdf.

Worthington, Ian, Monder Ram, Harvinder Boyal, and Mayank Shah. "Researching the Drivers of Socially Responsible Purchasing: A Cross-National Study of Supplier Diversity Initiatives." *Journal of Business Ethics* 79, no. 3 (2008): 319–331.

Zakrzewski, Anna, Kedra Newsom Reeves, Michael Kahlich, Maximilian Klein, Andrea Real Mattar, and Stephan Knobel. "Managing the Next Decade of Women's Wealth." Boston Consulting Group, April 9, 2020. https://www.bcg.com/publications /2020/managing-next-decade-women-wealth.

Zarya, Valentina. "These 10 Male Executives Are Committed to Reaching Gender Parity in 5 Years." *Fortune,* January 22, 2016. https://fortune.com/2016/01/22/he forshe-impact-champions/.

Index

Pages in italics indicate illustrations.